Preface

The preparation of these study manuals has been an exciting team adventure. It has been my privilege over the past few years to produce a number of books dealing with the subjects of discipleship, ministry and leadership. This has found a particular focus in two major volumes; *The Foundations of Christian Living* and *Master Builders,* both published by Sovereign World International. This material has become a major focus of our whole ministry and today those two volumes are published in a number of different languages.

Recently it has become even more clear that there is a growing need for material which will help Christians grow in life and develop in ministry. All over the world there is a phenomenal growth in numbers of new believers. Amongst more established believers there is a new hunger to progress in maturity both in life and in understanding of their faith.

These volumes are offered as part of the answer to this growing need. They began life as a pilot scheme devised by the leader of our team in the Netherlands, Kees de Vlieger. The effect throughout many churches and in the lives of many believers has been profound. Now they have been revised, remodelled and expanded, in the confidence that they will reach a much wider market and meet a much greater area of need.

I am so grateful to the team who have helped get them this far, in particular, to Kees de Vlieger for his inspiration. Andrew Whitman helped with the completion of certain study notes and his wife Rosie and Anne Holmes did a good job with the final proof reading. Simon Smailus, who prepared the manuals for their final production, deserves a special mention for the many dedicated hours he has put in compiling and correcting the text ready for final printing.

The last word must go, of course, to God our Father without whose help and blessing none of this would ever happen.

Bob Gordon

If you enjoy this book and would like to help us to send a copy
of it and many other titles to needy pastors in the **Third World**,
please write for further information
or send your gift to:

**Sovereign World Trust
PO Box 777, Tonbridge
Kent TN11 0ZS
United Kingdom**

or to the **'Sovereign World'** distributor in your country.

If sending money from outside the United Kingdom, please
send an International Money Order or Foreign Bank Draft in
STERLING, drawn on a **UK** bank to
Sovereign World Trust.

Contents

Introduction

This is the second of three manuals which have been produced together to provide a progressive and interesting study guide to growth in Christian life and ministry. The first focuses on certain basic essentials for personal Christian life and growth. The second considers some important lessons if we are to be effective in our ministry for Jesus. The third examines vital insights with regard to our call as servants of the Kingdom of God.

The goal of this particular study is to equip believers for their ministry.

The first four chapters present the elements which together form the foundation of a powerful ministry; i.e. *love, brokenness and having a servant heart, holiness and spiritual warfare*. These are followed by a few sections about the *gifts of the Holy Spirit* and how to stimulate personal growth in that area. The last three chapters discuss subjects like *prayer, faith* and *anointing*, which are so important if we are to live in the dynamic and power of the Holy Spirit.

These days there is a renewed interest and desire to serve in the same power and authority as the early Christians did in the book of Acts. The words of Jesus Himself are a great incentive to be engaged in ministry like this. In John 14:12 He says:

> *'I tell you the truth, anyone who has faith in me will do what I have been doing. He will do even greater things than these, because I am going to the Father.'*

and in John 20:21:

> *'As the Father has sent me, I am sending you.'*

The secret of all Christian service is knowing Jesus Christ and His ministry personally. It is our prayer that we will all glorify the Father by bearing much fruit in the ministry of Jesus!

Bob Gordon
Kees de Vlieger
and Team

How to make the most of this manual

There are two ways in which this manual can be used:

1. **Individually**
    This is working through the sections at your own pace at home. There are twelve sections and it is suggested that you complete one section a week.

2. **As a group**
    If you intend to use this manual for group study then we recommend that you purchase a copy of the *Leaders Manual* which has been specifically designed for this purpose. The *Leaders Manual* gives clear instructions on how to make the most of this material. It shows what material to teach each week and what homework to set. This is done by a detailed twelve-week plan contained in the *Leaders Manual*.

Some recommendations

*   Before you start the manual ask yourself the question; 'Do I really want to be a true disciple of Jesus?' If you do, then it is important to take this course seriously and to commit yourself to finishing it. Look ahead and see yourself as God desires you to be, and how you can be more fruitful in your service for Him. Determine to grow in your maturity in Christ.

*   Do not approach the study in a hurried way. Take your time in looking up the Scripture and answering the questions, especially if you are studying this course alone. Commit each teaching unit to the Lord in prayer and ask God to speak to you through it. Meditate upon relevant sections and try to apply the truths learned to your daily life. This is how to grow in maturity as a disciple of Jesus.

- If you are studying this course as part of a group, determine to be an integral part of that group. The word *fellowship* comes from the Greek word **koinonia** which means *to share things in common.* Your growth as a disciple of Jesus will be greatly helped by the encouragement that others can be to you. Learn to trust them and then share your life with them. Share with others in the group the things you are learning about God and His Word. In this way you will be able to live together in much of what you study and so your faith will increase and you will grow in your maturity in Christ.

- As one of a group you will get most out of the course by reading and studying the teaching unit well before the group actually meets together. This will give you time to meditate on the various truths and begin to apply them to your life. Questions arising can then be discussed and the truths more readily understood as the leader of the group progresses through the teaching unit as he feels led of God.

SECTION 1
Love

Introduction

I nvolvement in church work carries with it the danger of getting into all kinds of activities. This may lead to activism, resulting in the work becoming a bore – there is no joy in doing it, and there are no signs of fruit 'that remains'. God's first requirement is to know Him and to love Him.

> *'For I desire mercy, not sacrifice, and acknowledgement of God rather than burnt offerings.'* (Hosea 6:6)

When the work within the church is carried out without love, it will have negative side-effects, like these mentioned below:

- the right motivation is missing
- it will turn into activism
- it will not give peace, satisfaction or fruit
- there is a chance for rivalry and division
- it may disturb our relationship with God
- the ministry will be lacking in power
- God's love will not be communicated

In this section we will discuss the importance of love as the basis for a powerful ministry to the glory of God.

Key Verses

Deuteronomy 6:5

Romans 13:8–10

1 Corinthians 13:1–13

1 John 4:7–21

1 John 3:1–24

1 Peter 4:8

Matthew 22:36–40

Ephesians 3:14–19

PART 1.1
What is Love?

L ove is a dynamic reality. Love is personal and it is shown by what we do. In chapter 4 of his first letter John writes as follows:

'God is love. Whoever lives in love lives in God, and God in him.' (1 John 4:16b)

'This is how God showed His love among us: He sent His one and only Son into the world that we might live through Him ... that He loved us and sent His Son as an atoning sacrifice for our sins.' (1 John 4:9 & 10)

Love brings reconciliation and new life!

Aspects of love

In the Greek language there are four words which express various aspects of love. In the New Testament, the first is never used, the second is barely used at all, the third is used with increasing frequency, and the fourth is the New Testament's 'special word'.

- *Eros* – This is sexual love or desire. It is the romantic kind of love which God created beautiful and pure but which now, due to the Fall, can lead to lust. This word is not used in the New Testament.

Personal Notes

- *Storge* –This is used to specify family love, and occurs only in its negative form, e.g. in Romans 1:31 where Paul bemoans the absence of this attribute.

- *Philia* – This kind of love stems from a particular relationship, e.g. family members, relatives, friends, church members. At the heart of this word is the idea of 'affection' and 'friendship'.

- *Agape* – This is a love that is directed towards another person rather than towards oneself. It is the word used in the New Testament when it speaks of the special love that is released within us by the Holy Spirit, e.g. Romans 5:5.

Agape love is the love God displays towards us. It is a love which does not seek itself, and is unconditional. God showed us what this word really means by sending His Son into this world and letting Him die in our place.

God wants us to have the same love for each other. In the church at Corinth this *agape love* was not functioning. In 1 Corinthians 13 Paul explains what this love means.

> *'Love is patient, love is kind. It does not envy, it does not boast, it is not proud. It is not rude, it is not self-seeking, it is not easily angered, it keeps no record of wrongs. Love does not delight in evil but rejoices with the truth. It always protects, always trusts, always hopes, always perseveres. Love never fails.'*　　(1 Corinthians 13:4–8)

What do these words mean?

- *patient*: long-suffering, being able to put up with continued difficulty for a long time before getting angry.

- *kind*: gentle, interested in the happiness and feelings of others, merciful.

- *not envious*: not having a grudging desire for or feeling discontent at the sight of another's excellence or advantages, not jealous.

- *not boastful*: does not show off, brag, swagger.

- *not proud*: not haughty, not puffed up; does not make things look bigger than they are, but is honest.

- ***not rude***: does not abuse, but is sensitive.

- ***not self-seeking***: not ambitious or proud; not seeking self-interest but loving one's neighbour as oneself.

- ***not easily angered***: does not allow feelings of hate, or bear grudges.

- ***keeps no record of wrongs***: does not blame, does not seek retaliation.

- ***does not delight in evil but rejoices with the truth***.

- ***it always protects***: does not reveal other people's mistakes, gives security, and shields from injury.

- ***always trusts***: has confidence in others, gives assurance.

- ***always hopes***: creates anticipation, confidence and a goal.

- ***always perseveres***: is always effective and powerful, is eternal, remains loyal to the end.

It was this love which compelled Paul to live for God (2 Corinthians 5:14, 15).

We receive this love when we open ourselves to the Spirit of God (Romans 5:5).

When we receive this love it will show itself in practical ways like:

- we will love others (1 John 4:11)

- it will lead to action (1 John 3:18)

- we will obey God's commands (1 John 5:3)

- it will build the church (Ephesians 3:14–19)

- we will remain in God (John 14:15–20)

- it will bear witness to the world (John 13:34–35)

- it will glorify the Father (John 15:8)

PART 1.2
The Importance of Love

Love is the soil in the Kingdom of God.

> *'If I have the gift of prophecy and can fathom all mysteries and all knowledge, and if I have faith that can move mountains, but have not love, I am nothing. If I give all I possess to the poor and surrender my body to the flames, but have not love, I gain nothing.'*
>
> (1 Corinthians 13:2–3)

We can display all the gifts of the Holy Spirit, but if they are not shown and ministered in love, then they are as nothing. The most important thing is that we grow in love.

> *'Love never fails. But where there are prophecies, they will cease.'* (1 Corinthians 13:8)

The gifts of the Spirit should be the means by which we express God's love. If we concentrate on the gifts of the Spirit only and forget what they actually have been given for, we will miss God's purpose. Gifts are given in the first place to point people to Jesus and build up the Church. In the Bible the passages on the gifts of the Holy Spirit are always balanced by passages on love (e.g. in Romans 12). They go hand in hand. Power and gifts without love are dangerous. The gifts may only be exercised to express God's love.

> *Love for God and others should be the motivating force behind all our work for God.*

PART 1.3
Those That Love the Lord Have Many Blessings

G od chose to work together with man on the basis of a relationship, an agreement. This is called a covenant. In the Old Testament there are many examples of God entering into a covenant with man. In the New Testament there is the new covenant through the blood of Christ. All these covenants have the following important characteristics in common:

- it is God's choice

- it is possible only through the blood of atonement

- all people involved must submit to the rules of the covenant

- God promises to bless His people

These blessings include the following:

- God is faithful, keeping His covenant of love to a thousand generations of those who love Him and keep His commands (Deuteronomy 7:9)

- God's goodness and love will follow them (Psalm 23:6)

- God watches over them (Psalm 145:20)

- God lets Himself be found by those who seek Him (Proverbs 8:17)

- all things work together for good to those who love God (Romans 8:28)

- God lives in them (1 John 4:16)

In practice, we experience rather the opposite at times, namely trouble, conflict, persecution, suffering etc. It is true that these also come to God's children, *but nothing will separate us from the love of Christ*. (Refer also to Psalm 23 and Romans 8:31–39.)

Personal Notes

PART 1.4
Ways to Receive God's Love

- By being open to God. He will build His love into our lives (1 Thessalonians 3:12).

- By knowing God in increasing measure (1 John 4:7–12). We do this by spending time with Him; praying, listening, seeking and worshipping etc.

- By understanding God's commands, and then obeying them out of love for Him (John 14:15, 21).

- By the Holy Spirit (Romans 5:5; Galatians 5:22).

- By making a conscious choice for God's love and pursuing it (Colossians 3:12–14).

- By praying for each other (Ephesians 3:14–19).

  'Flee the evil desires of youth, and pursue righteousness, faith, love and peace, along with those who call on the Lord out of a pure heart.'   (2 Timothy 2:22)

God helps us to love Him because we do not have this love in ourselves. In other words: God loves us deeply, despite our feelings. He helps us also to love other Christians, and to love the people in the world who do not know Him, that they may be brought to Jesus and experience His love for themselves.

PART 1.5
What Makes God's Love Function?

In 1 Timothy 1:3–7 Paul shows us three requirements for being able to operate in God's love (verse 5). These three requirements are:

i) A pure heart

Before God can give us of Himself our hearts must be cleansed. When we have pure hearts we will forgive and love others. Purity opens our lives for the fruit of the Spirit. We must keep coming before God, confessing our sins and being purified by the power of the blood of Jesus.

ii) A good conscience

Our conscience needs to be at peace. When it condemns us we have crossed a boundary. Our conscience is God's alarm bell and when it wakes us up we realise that our relationship with God is disturbed. This robs us of our confidence. We need to have a clear conscience as this enables us to come boldly into God's presence, to receive His love and pass it on.

iii) A sincere faith

We are to live by faith.

> *'Without faith it is impossible to please God.'*
> (Hebrews 11:6)

Only by faith will we be able to live the way God wants us to live. We need to trust wholly in God and let go of our own human securities. This means giving God control over our lives. When we surrender ourselves to God like this in faith, God's love will become manifest in and through our lives.

PART 1.6
Ways That Show Our Love for God

- *We will rejoice over who God is*
  God the Father is a God of love, forgiveness, mercy, faithfulness, justice etc. (Psalm 103:8–13).

- *We will give thanks to God for all He has done for us*
  In His love God has done mighty deeds. Out of love He sent His Son and opened a way for us to become part of His Kingdom and to actually become His children (1 John 3:1).

- *We will get to know God better*
  Especially as we read and meditate on His Word and fellowship with Him in prayer (Hosea 6:3).

- *We will obey God's Word and His commands* (John 14:15)

- *We will tell Him that we love Him*

- *We will commit ourselves totally to God* (John 21:15–17)

- *We will love our brothers and even our enemies*
  Agape love is determined to seek the other's best (Romans 13:8–13; Galatians 6:10).

Summary and Application

1. Agape love is God's unconditional love.

2. Without love everything we do is worthless (1 Corinthians 13:1–3).

3. When we know God personally we will love Him and love others as well (1 John 4:7).

4. The Bible calls us to imitate Christ in His love (Ephesians 5:1–2).

5. Love is shown by the actions it prompts.

6. Love builds the Body of Christ.

7. Loving God brings many blessings.

8. *'Do everything in love'* (1 Corinthians 16:14).

Assignment

Together discuss the following verses from the book of Deuteronomy:

1. Deuteronomy 4:37
    Who is the first to give love? _____

    _____

    What proves it? _____

    _____

2. Deuteronomy 6:5
    What does the Lord ask of us? _____

    _____

3. Deuteronomy 7:7–9
    Who is the loving one in verses 7–8? _____

    _____

    Who shows love in verse 9? _____

    _____

    When this love relationship between God and man is mutual, it is the basis for all blessings.

4. Deuteronomy 13:1–3
    Why does God sometimes test us? _____

    _____

5. Deuteronomy 15:16
    What is the reason this slave does not want to leave his master?

    _____

    _____

6. Deuteronomy 23:5
   What did the Lord do to protect His people? _____

   _____

   Why? _____

   _____

7. Deuteronomy 30:6
   Are we able to love God of ourselves? _____

   _____

   What needs to happen first of all? _____

   _____

8. Deuteronomy 30:19–20
   Love requires us to make a choice! Why? _____

   _____

   Now make a personal decision. Do you choose to love the Lord with all your heart, with all your soul and with all your strength?

   ○ Yes

   ○ No

   Love for God is the foundation of our ministry. We will have to show in practice whether our love for God is sincere or not. Jesus was tested on this point, and the following Bible Study, **'The Test for the Ministry'**, will examine our hearts on this as well.

Bible Study: *The Test for the Ministry*

T o be admitted into God's service is a great privilege. However, the devil is not pleased when we serve God, and therefore will try to stop us. He will do this through trials and temptations. God Himself does not tempt us, but He does allow temptation to test our love for Him. We see this in the life of Jesus. As soon as He had been filled with the Holy Spirit and started His earthly ministry, Jesus was faced with temptations. Matthew 4:1–11 tells how Jesus was led into the wilderness *'to be tempted by the devil.'*

Answer the following questions. After you finish you may check them with the answers at the end of this study.

1. By whom was Jesus led into the desert according to Matthew 4:1?

    _____

    _____

2. Read Hebrews 4:15–16 and describe why Jesus had to experience temptations:

    _____

    _____

    The temptations which we may have to face will be of the same nature as those experienced by Jesus in the desert. Starting a ministry without knowing the victory in Christ in these temptations is a risky affair.

3. *The circumstances* (Matthew 4:2–4)
    Jesus had not had any food for forty days and forty nights (see verse 3). A first temptation may come through the circumstances in which we find ourselves. Difficult situations, set-backs, struggles, hunger, persecution, loneliness etc. may well be part of our ministry (refer also to 2 Corinthians 11:24–29).

How does satan attack us in these circumstances (either directly or, more often than not, indirectly through the cravings of our sinful nature)?

_____

_____

_____

In our own circumstances satan often sows doubts: *'If...'* He will make you doubt the fact that:

- God is your Father

- the Father will provide

- you have a calling

Satan tried to tempt Jesus into using His power for His own ends in this particular situation: *'Tell these stones...'*

Especially in difficult circumstances there is a great danger of taking control over matters rather than trusting God continually in obedience.

4. What was Jesus' response in this situation? (Matthew 4:4). Describe this in your own words.

_____

_____

_____

_____

Later on (in Matthew 6:31–33) Jesus explained this to His disciples. Is this the faith-attitude of your heart, or do you have difficulties in this area?

_____

_____

_____

Personal Notes

5. ***Success, miracles, power*** (Matthew 4:5–7)
Jesus was next tempted to show His miraculous powers. Temptation in ministry can come when there is apparent success and great miracles are taking place; perhaps no miraculous things are happening as yet, but you have set your heart on it; or you may be envious of someone else's successful ministry. In that case your heart is not focused on God's will, but on a making a name for yourself. What is the warning given in Matthew 7:21–23?

_____

_____

_____

6. Satan used a word from the Bible to tempt Jesus. Jesus recognised this. How did He overcome in this temptation?

_____

_____

_____

Jesus did not want to promote or please Himself. Read John 5:30, 41 and define the one desire that Jesus had:

_____

_____

_____

Is this your desire as well?

_____

_____

7. ***Power, dominion and possession*** (Matthew 4:8–10)
Satan showed Jesus everything He would be given if only He would worship him. He would get power, dominion, possessions etc. However, it was not God's will for Jesus to receive these things from satan; they would be His only by way of the cross (Philippians 2:5–11).

Many defeated leaders owe their downfall to having yielded to the temptations of pride, money and sex. This may be due to a strong desire to assert oneself, caused by having a craving for these things in one's heart. Even today satan tries to trip up leaders in these things. How did Jesus overcome?

_____

_____

_____

Jesus did not come to rule, to assert or to prove Himself, but to serve. He put aside all His own ambitions, all His desires etc. Read again Philippians 2:5–11.

What is your attitude regarding this?

_____

_____

_____

8. In 1 John 2:16 we find the essence of these three temptations. Summarise by filling in the blanks:

   'For everything in the world – the _____

   _____ *,*

   the _____

   and the _____

   _____ *– comes not from the Father*

   but from the world.'

9. These temptations will come up against you, in whatever way you seek to serve God. In trying to trip us up satan will use the same tricks time and again. Read 1 Corinthians 10:13. What three facts emerge from this verse?

   a) _____

   b) _____

   c) _____

10. Reflect once again on the three temptations mentioned in Matthew 4 and the summary in 1 John 2:16.

    You may discover elements in your heart as well that are hindering the love of God in your life. Confess them to God and resist them in the name of Jesus and with the Word.

    Jesus had decided that He only wanted to do the will of the Father, to glorify Him and to love Him. Now pray a simple prayer. Let this be a personal covenant that you are making at this time with your heavenly Father:

    _____

    _____

    _____

    _____

Answers

1. By the Spirit of God.

2. Jesus experienced temptation firstly so He can identify with us when we are tempted, and secondly so He can help us when we are tempted.

3. First he tries to make us doubt, and then tries to tempt us into doing things in our own strength: *'Tell these stones...'*

4. Jesus used a word from Deuteronomy 8:3 and made it clear to satan that the issue at stake is not the situation in which one finds oneself, but the word of God in that situation.

    Personal

5. It is not what you do that matters most, however special it may be; what matters is who you are in Christ; whether you love God and seek to do His will.

6. Jesus again used a word from Scripture to defeat satan (Deuteronomy 6:16). Jesus rejected using a verse to vindicate His own desires and ambitions.

    Jesus did not seek praise from men, but sought to do the Father's will. He always did what pleased the Father.

    Personal

7. Jesus was not swayed by personal ambitions, He was not wanting to rule and have power in a worldly sense. He worshipped God, His Father, only.

    Personal

8. cravings of sinful man (cf. Question 3); lust of his eyes (cf. Question 5); boasting of what he has and does (cf. Question 7).

9. a)   No temptation will be beyond what you can bear.
    b)   God is faithful.
    c)   He will provide a way out, will give victory.

10. Personal

SECTION 2
Brokenness and Having a Servant Heart

Introduction

Key Verses

PART 2.1   The Example of Jesus

PART 2.2   Simplicity of Spirit

PART 2.3   Ointment Poured Forth

PART 2.4   The Mark of God

PART 2.5   The Nature of a Servant

Bible Study
Spiritual Leaders

Introduction

A vital aspect of a spiritual ministry is brokenness. In John 12:24 Jesus says:

> *'I tell you the truth, unless a grain of wheat falls to the ground and dies, it remains only a single seed. But if it dies, it produces many seeds.'*

We energetic Christians so often get in God's way with things like:

- our opinion that we are *something*
- our own strength and talents, our strong points
- personal desires, interests or pride
- our striving
- an independent, fleshly attitude

There is no limit to God, but often we give Him so little room to work in and through our lives. Much of our Christian life and work is really the old fleshly life.

This is not what God desires. God really cannot use **somethings**. It is in the lives of those who are described in Scripture as being **nothing** that God has chosen to manifest His power and glory (1 Corinthians 1:28, 29). We need a deep inner awareness that we will have to let go of many things we previously counted as valuable. If we are to see and know the power of God we need to die to ourselves in a radical way.

We are all well aware of the fact that much in our lives needs to change if we want to know the power of God as He intended.

Key Verses

Genesis 32:22–32   Isaiah 57:15

1 Corinthians 1:27–29   James 4:10

Galatians 2:20   2 Corinthians 12:9–10

Philippians 2:5–11   Philippians 3:4–11

PART 2.1
The Example of Jesus

Brokenness became a way of life for Jesus long before He saw the cross. Of course, Jesus truly was somebody – He was the Son of God, but He emptied Himself (Philippians 2:6–7). Here was Jesus, the perfect man, who knew the ways of God's power in an immediate and personal sense: He brought life out of death more than once during His earthly ministry; when He touched men, they were made well; when He spoke, demons trembled and fled. We can see the secret of God's power in the experience of Jesus (John 3:34). We receive the Spirit of God only by measure, although the Father is willing to fill us to overflowing. The measure with which we open ourselves up determines the measure of the Holy Spirit within us. Hurts, pride, selfishness and rebellion often prevent the Holy Spirit from having room to work within us. Within the heart of Jesus there was no darkness. In Jesus' heart there was room for the Father to pour in the Spirit without measure.

We need to understand that this was the very way by which Jesus lived and manifested the power of God. He became nothing!

PART 2.2
Simplicity of Spirit

'Blessed are the poor in spirit, for theirs is the kingdom of heaven.'   (Matthew 5:3)

In this verse Jesus speaks about spiritual *poverty*. By this He means a spiritual attitude of dependence and simplicity.

By nature we have an independent and wilful attitude, which causes us to act from our own fleshly strength. Yet God wants to teach us, through a process of brokenness, to be completely dependent on Him. This is simplicity of spirit, which makes us strong in God.

In the Bible we find many examples of people who had learned to trust God in a humble and simple way. One example is Mary in Luke 1:26–38.

Jesus Himself lived and served in this simple, yet powerful way.

In Matthew 14:13–21, for example, Jesus multiplied the bread and fishes. In verse 19 we read:

'...and looking up to heaven...'

To perform this miracle He was completely dependent on His Father and in a simple, childlike manner He trusted Him fully.

'For the eyes of the Lord range throughout the earth to strengthen those whose hearts are fully committed to Him.'   (2 Chronicles 16:9)

'This is what the Sovereign LORD, the Holy One of Israel, says: "In repentance and rest is your salvation, in quietness and trust is your strength."'   (Isaiah 30:15)

Our heavenly Father wants us to be fruitful, but before this can happen we need to realise that we are nothing in ourselves, that we are unable to do this by ourselves and are solely dependent on God.

This could seem to be a very negative thing, when we hear in a deep way that we are nothing and that God wants us to be nothing. In fact it could crush our spirits and lead us into a tremendous sense of condemnation. This is just what the devil would delight to do in our lives. However, this is not what the Father wants to do.

PART 2.3
Ointment Poured Forth

When Mary anointed the feet of Jesus (John 12:1–8), the jar had to be broken before the ointment could flow out. The value of this oil amounted to about a year's wages. Only after the jar was broken could the fragrance fill the whole house. In a similar way, we need to be broken before the ointment of the Holy Spirit can flow out from us and the fragrance of Christ can spread (2 Corinthians 2:14–16).

Personal Notes

PART 2.4
The Mark of God

Read Genesis 32:22–32. Here we read about the meeting between God and Jacob. Jacob met God face to face. In God's eyes this was the making of Jacob's new life. After this Jacob was not the same any longer, because he bore the mark of God in his body. There was a lameness about the new Jacob (or Israel), but his lameness became his strength. We also need to meet with God, to be touched by the power of God and to be burdened by the holiness of God.

True brokenness is:

- *knowing that God has looked into our lives*
- *realising that in His love He has spared us*

Brokenness like that is not weakness, it is the very source of strength in the spirit. After such a meeting with God things never look the same again. There is nothing stronger than a man who has been touched by God. He has nothing left to prove and nothing more to fear. The old fight has been laid to rest. Inside there is an emptiness that only God can fill. Outwardly there is a weakness which only God can make strong.

> *'I have been crucified with Christ and I no longer live, but Christ lives in me. The life I live in the body, I live by faith in the Son of God, who loved me and gave Himself for me.'* (Galatians 2:20)

We need to live like this if we are to be really effective for God and bear *'fruit that remains'*.

We cannot force brokenness ourselves – only God can do this if we yield our lives to Him. It is a daily process of obedience and humble service.

PART 2.5
The Nature of a Servant

One of the fruits of brokenness is that we are willing to serve God freely. A servant of God is one who has dethroned himself and everything else in his life or experience, and enthroned Jesus, making Him Lord of all his life. He puts Jesus first in everything. This means that we will put God's Kingdom first in our lives (Matthew 6:33), and not riches, power, possessions or anything else (Matthew 6:24).

A servant:

- seeks first the Kingdom of God (Matthew 6:33)

- serves others and in doing so serves the Lord Jesus (Matthew 25:31–40)

- is willing to deny himself, take up his cross and follow Jesus (Luke 9:23)

- knows that it is more blessed to give than to receive (Acts 20:33–35)

- is faithful when entrusted with something (Matthew 25:21)

- helps to carry the burdens of others (Galatians 6:2)

- is humble, gentle, patient and bears with others in love (Ephesians 4:2)

- looks to the interest of others (Philippians 2:3–4)

- wants to please his Lord (2 Timothy 2:4)

God hates pride and arrogance (Proverbs 8:13). He desires us to walk humbly with Him (Micah 6:8).

> *'Humble yourselves, therefore, under God's mighty hand, that He may lift you up in due time.'*   (1 Peter 5:6)

We need to humble ourselves. This is not grovelling about in the dust. Rather, we realise that in ourselves we are nothing, and that we need God to reign in our hearts. He will make us strong and will raise us up at the right time. We need to trust God. This is what it means to have the nature of a servant.

Jesus said:

> *'Take my yoke upon you and learn from me, for I am gentle and humble in heart, and you will find rest for your souls. For my yoke is easy and my burden is light.'*
> (Matthew 11:29, 30)

We can learn humility from Jesus by following His example. He said of Himself:

> **'But I am among you as one who serves.'** (Luke 22:27)

Summary and Application

1. The only people whom God can use effectively are those who have been broken before Him like Jesus.

2. We need to die to ourselves in a radical way.

3. A disciple of Jesus has a great deal of potential for God, but this will only be realised if he gives God access to his life to work out His will.

4. Our strong points are often, in God's eyes, our weak points.

5. A true servant of God is one who puts God first in everything and serves Him only.

Thus *love* and ***brokenness*** produce the basis for ministry and leadership within a church.

The love of God builds us up in God's strength. Brokenness breaks down our own strength, so that God's power can be made perfect in our weakness.

The following Bible Study, **'Spiritual Leaders'**, will work this out further.

Bible Study: *Spiritual Leaders*

I n this Bible Study we will discuss some general principles in regard to leadership within the Christian Church. These principles are equally true for each church member, as all of us are concerned with leadership to some degree.

Complete the following assignments. After answering all the questions you may check them with the answers at the end of the study.

1.   Leaders are appointed by God. One example from the Old Testament is Moses. In Exodus 3:1–12 we read that Moses is called to lead the people.

Stephen also describes this calling of Moses in Acts 7:35. Whose authority did Moses receive at this calling?

_____

_____

Who was this Angel (in Exodus 3:2)?

_____

_____

Even though he had this particular calling and authority, it was not God's intention that Moses should handle this task alone. Read Exodus 18:13–18 and state why not:

_____

_____

_____

What did Moses need to learn as a leader?

_____

_____

_____

2. God's intention for us is to learn to delegate. In Exodus
    18:21–23 we find an example of this. God wants to involve
    other people as well. What did He tell Moses to do?

    _____

    _____

    _____

3. What was the effect going to be on:

    a) the life of Moses?

        _____

        _____

    b) the leaders?

        _____

        _____

    c) all of the people?

        _____

        _____

4. It is clear that it was God's will that others should assist
    Moses in leading the people. The people to be appointed
    by Moses had to meet certain requirements, had to possess
    certain qualities. In verse 21 *four qualities* are mentioned,
    namely:

    a) _____

    b) _____

    c) _____

    d) _____

5.   The first quality mentioned is ***to be capable***. This does not mean they had to be strong physically. What do you think is meant by this word *capable*? (Refer also to Genesis 47:3–6; 2 Chronicles 26:15.)

_____

_____

_____

Enthusiasm is not the first requirement, as this does not necessarily indicate somebody's competence. We see the same thing in business: a person is not just accepted because of his enthusiasm, but because of his capacities to fulfil a certain task. (Refer also to 2 Timothy 2:2.)

6.   The second quality is ***to be God-fearing***. The first quality was *capability*. When we stress capability only we may end up with a spiritual worker who does not meet the demands of his job after all. Read Psalm 111:10 and Proverbs 1:7 and state why the *'fear of the Lord'* is needed:

_____

_____

_____

_____

7.   The third quality mentioned is ***to be trustworthy***. A church worker must be reliable and incorruptible. This implies loyalty and sincerity towards other co-workers and leaders. Why is this so important, especially as regards to the calling and the vision of the church? (Refer also to 2 Timothy 2:2.)

_____

_____

_____

_____

8. The fourth quality is *to hate dishonest gain*. This does not just refer to money. It has more to do with the attitude of our hearts. It is a great temptation to do something for your own personal gain. Besides money this could be honour, reputation, a high position or self-complacency. Define this fourth quality in your own words. (Refer also to 1 Peter 5:2.)

    _____

    _____

    _____

    _____

9. Do you possess the four qualities that have been mentioned?

    O   Yes

    O   No

    O   In part

    What are you going to do about this?

    _____

    _____

    _____

10. In Mark 10:35–45 Jesus teaches His disciples something important about the attitude of a leader. What is the desire of James and John (verses 35–37)?

    _____

    _____

    _____

    Who is leadership for (verse 40)?

    _____

    _____

What is the prerequisite if one is to receive this (verses 42–45)?

_____

_____

_____

Do you find it difficult to be a servant?

O   Yes

O   No

11. In Acts 6:1–7 we see that the disciples were confronted with new demands which they were not able to handle themselves. Therefore they had to get new people involved. Which were the qualities these seven men had to have (verse 3)?

a)   _____

b)   _____

Stephen was one of the people chosen. Apart from the qualities mentioned above he displayed some others as well (see verses 5 and 8). What were they?

c) _____

d) _____

e) _____

Nobody is perfect and if we have to wait until we are, we will never be able to do a thing. Referring to Acts chapter 6 however, to what should you give attention, in order to be an effective co-worker?

_____

_____

_____

_____

Answers

1. God's authority, through the angel who appeared to him. In the Old Testament the appearance of the Lord is a revelation of Jesus Christ (refer also to Judges 6:11–24; 13:1–18; Daniel 3:24, 25).

    Moses would wear himself out completely, it was too heavy for him.

    That it is not good to handle everything alone. He had to learn to delegate.

2. To select other men and appoint them as officials over thousands, hundreds, fifties and tens.

3. a) It would make his load lighter; he would be able to stand the strain.
    b) The leaders would share the load with Moses.
    c) The people would go home satisfied.

4. a) To be capable.
    b) To be God-fearing.
    c) To be trustworthy.
    d) To hate dishonest gain.

5. Being competent, dedicated, brave.

6. It is the beginning of wisdom. This is needed to make the right decisions and to be able to administer justice.

7. If this attitude is not present then the chances for division and splitting up are great. One cannot give responsibility to a person who is unreliable or who does not have a good reputation.

8. *For example*: not concerned with personal gain; your main concern is God's honour and His Kingdom.

9. Personal

10. To sit at Jesus' side in His Kingdom.

    For whom it has been prepared; it is a gift from God.

    To be willing to be a servant.

    Personal

11. a) Known to be full of the Spirit.
    b) Full of wisdom.

    c) Full of faith and of the Holy Spirit.
    d) Full of God's grace and power.
    e) Did great wonders and miraculous signs.

    Personal

SECTION 3
Holiness

Introduction

God is holy! This is being revealed to us continually by the Holy Spirit and by Scripture (Isaiah 6:3; 1 Peter 1:16). In fact the Bible mentions God's holiness as much as His love.

In Hebrew the word used for holy is **Qâdosh**, which means:

- holy
- pure
- set apart
- dedicated to
- different, other

Holiness means separation; being set apart from all that is sinful, impure and unclean, and being dedicated to God.

God is holy. This means:

- He is perfect
- He is clean, pure
- He is almighty
- He is the Most High

He is worthy of our praise, so we need to approach Him with reverence and awe. When God, the Holy One, reveals Himself, what we see is His magnificence, His glory (Exodus 24:16–17; John 1:14).

Key Verses

Leviticus 11:44–45   Matthew 3:11–14

Ephesians 1:4   1 Thessalonians 4:3–8

2 Corinthians 7:1   Hebrews 12:28–29

PART 3.1
God Wants Us to Live Holy Lives

As disciples of Jesus we are called to be different (1 Peter 1:15, 16; Ephesians 1:17–20). We belong to God's family and therefore should live holy lives. We are children of God the Father and as such we need to exhibit the family characteristics (Hebrews 12:10; 1 Peter 2:9).

In the New Testament the Church is considered to be the family of God. It is God's desire to reveal Himself to the world through the Church. The Church is to bear testimony to God's:

- manifold wisdom (Ephesians 3:10)

- love (Ephesians 3:18, 19)

- glory (Ephesians 3:21)

- mighty acts (1 Peter 2:9; Psalm 145:4)

If the life of the Church is pure it will exhibit God's character, His holiness.

That is why it is important that there is love and unity among God's children. This will show other people that we belong to God's family.

> '*By this all men will know that you are my disciples, **if you love one another**.*'   (John 13:35)

PART 3.2
What is Sanctification in Practical Terms?

Sanctification is being separated to God and separated from evil things and ways. It is the manifestation of the life of the Holy Spirit within us when we enter into relationship with God through faith in Jesus. God's plan is to transform us into the likeness of His Son (Romans 8:29). This has important personal consequences (1 John 2:3–6).

In Leviticus 19:1–18 God shows us that holiness has to do with the practice of our daily living. This is summarised in verse 18 as follows:

> '...but love your neighbour as yourself.'

PART 3.3
How Our Sanctification Takes Place

It is God's purpose that we should be sanctified through Christ's sacrifice (Ephesians 1:4). This is a granted sanctification, which nevertheless implies a personal responsibility.

We are charged to walk as Jesus did (1 John 2:6), to obey God's commands (Deuteronomy 26:16–19) and to put on the new self, created to be like God in true righteousness and holiness (Ephesians 4:24). Our obedience to this, through the power of the Holy Spirit, enables this process of sanctification in which both God and man are involved.

In Leviticus 20:8 the Lord says:

> 'I am the LORD, who makes you holy.'

And in verse 26 the Lord asks of us:

> 'You are to be holy to me, for I am holy.'

This process of sanctification is not by adhering to the letter of the law: *it is by faith!* The following points are important here:

i) Know your position in Christ

- In Christ we have received holiness (1 Corinthians 1:30)
- Christ sanctified Himself for us (John 17:19)
- The blood of Jesus sanctifies us (Hebrews 13:12)
- Jesus' obedience makes us holy (Hebrews 10:7, 10)

ii) Decide to be willing to be sanctified

- By making every effort to be holy (Hebrews 12:14)
- By being at God's service (Romans 6:19, 20)
- By purifying ourselves from everything that contaminates, and from works of the flesh (2 Corinthians 7:1)

iii) Let God work it out by His Spirit

- Let God's glory transform you (2 Corinthians 3:18)
- Let yourself be filled with God's Spirit and with fire (Matthew 3:11–12)

This process of sanctification starts when we behold God's glory (Exodus 34:5–10; Isaiah 6:1–8).

When we behold God's glory we are seeing a holy God manifesting His nature. Beholding God's glory will transform us progressively into His likeness so that we can increasingly reflect God's glory. The reason for this is that we begin to see who we really are in comparison with a holy God and so we desire changes in ourselves. When we yield ourselves to God He will come and make it possible. In this way we are transformed progressively into His likeness.

Personal Notes

PART 3.4
Encounter with God

Isaiah gives a powerful testimony to the holiness of God, and the impact it made on his life (Isaiah 6:1–8). These words of the prophet portray an experience that few of us have ever known. It was so deep, so rich and powerful that it brought about a radical change in his life. Each one of us needs a powerful experience like that.

God's desire is that we should get to know Him in this way. This experience of the holiness, depth and power of God is, through the Holy Spirit, open to all believers who will open their hearts and seek Him. God wants us to know what is in His heart. There we see His holiness, love, righteousness and justice. We need to feel His heartbeat, so that our own hearts will beat in time with His. Our hearts need to be stretched to comprehend as God comprehends and feel His passion for the lost.

Through Isaiah's testimony in Isaiah 6:1–8, we discover the following characteristics in such a meeting:

- it is an encounter with God (verse 1–2)

- it reveals God's holiness, His glory (verses 3–4)

- it reveals man's sin, his need (verse 5)

- it brings cleansing and reconciliation (verses 6, 7)

- it brings about a change in your life (verse 8)

- it makes you willing to live for God and to serve Him (verse 8)

Isaiah met the holy fire of God. It was a profound experience of the reality of God. It burned the dross and rubbish out of him. Only the purging touch of the angel in the mercy of God saved him. But for this touch of mercy he would have been finished. This is what we need in our discipleship and leadership. We need to know that we have come to the end of ourselves, that but for the grace of God we are absolutely lost. There is so much triviality and self-centeredness in our Christian experience. So many need to go on having ministry for deliverance from bondages and keep on asking for prayer because they have never touched the fire of God. Those who have touched the fire of God find their bonds are burned away. This brings real freedom.

This is what is involved in a proper conversion. Repentance is not just some ritual whereby we give our hearts to Jesus. It is God's holiness which convicts us of sin and changes the natural man. God's holiness can deliver us from a self-centered religious life. We need to catch such a vision of God in Jesus through the Spirit and be so radically changed that the old life no longer carries the appeal or power it had.

PART 3.5
Baptism of Fire

In Matthew 3:11 John the Baptist says:

> *'I baptise you with water for repentance. But after me will come one who is more powerful than I, whose sandals I am not fit to carry. He will baptise you with the Holy Spirit and with fire.'*

Through the Holy Spirit we receive a revelation of God in our lives, which means an encounter with God's love and holiness.

Apart from the fullness of the Spirit which we received through the baptism with the Holy Spirit, God also wants to send His fire into our lives to cleanse us.

This fire has the following effects:

- it sanctifies and cleanses us
- it removes from our lives all that is sinful and evil
- it makes us into the people that God wants us to be
- it fills us with God's love
- it sets us on fire for Jesus

Many people have not allowed God to do this work of purging and renewal in their lives. This is why so many are unchanged and are still so ineffective in their Christian lives when they should have been powerful and fruitful. We need to yield our lives ever afresh to God, meet with Him again and ask Him to keep filling us with His Holy Spirit.

PART 3.6
How to Receive the Baptism with Fire

- Realise your emptiness, impotence and dependence on God

- Thirst after God (Exodus 3:18; 34:5–10; Jeremiah 29:11–13)

- Be open to God; do not hold anything back and give Him all of yourself

- Allow God to fill you afresh or for the first time with His Holy Spirit (Luke 11:13; John 7:37–39; Ephesians 5:18)

- Let the blazing fire of the Holy Spirit go through your life and allow Him to purge you of everything that is not of God

- Remain obedient and open to God, so that God's fire may touch the lives of other people as well (Romans 12:11)

Conclusion

I t is not in us to turn to God and seek Him with all our hearts. What God does is begin to stir us by the Holy Spirit. Very often we do not recognise this as the hand of God, but God is nevertheless at work in us. He causes us to have a divine dissatisfaction in our hearts so that we will recognise that we need more of God and need to change in ourselves to become more like God. God uses many different means to rouse us from our contentment and complacency. It is impossible to say how God will move. He knows us and He knows the way to take us. He wants us to go on in our spiritual lives and He will do all He can to achieve this. However, God will not force us, we need to yield to His prompting in our hearts.

For a number of Christians the fire of God's Holy Spirit has gone cold. We need to ask God to rekindle the fire in our hearts. Then we need to feed this fire (2 Timothy 1:6). God can then begin again to consume the rubbish in our lives, so that we will become more like Jesus and serve Him more effectively.

Some Christians have never known the fire of God in their lives. If that is you, you need to ask God to baptise you with the Holy Spirit and with fire. Only if we have a raging fire of God within us can we start fires for God in other places.

Jesus was like this and so were many of the early disciples. We need to be the same in our day. When His fire comes upon us it acts to purge and change our lives, like heat being applied to a crucible of gold. This process takes time, but eventually we become holy and blameless (Ephesians 5:27). We will become what God wants us and needs us to be.

Application

1. Sanctification is the process that follows our new birth. Is there anything you can do personally to encourage this to happen? Choose one of the following possibilities:

   ○ By pursuing sanctification in your own strength

   ○ By regarding it impossible to live a holy life

   ○ By believing that you do not sin any more because you have died with Christ

   ○ By allowing the Holy Spirit to make you holy

   ○ By ...

2. Have you experienced the baptism with fire, by which the Holy Spirit purifies and renews you?

   ○ Yes

   ○ No

3. Perhaps you have experienced it but now the power of the Spirit in your life has gone. Do you long to have it again?

   ○ Yes

   ○ No

4. If you are already experiencing this renewal, do you long for more, or are you content with things as they are? Describe this:

   _____

   _____

   _____

5. Describe what has appealed to you most in this section.

   _____

   _____

   _____

What are you going to do with, or about, this?

_____

_____

_____

Knowing God's holiness and the baptism with His fire, will sanctify our lives from within. The result will be that we will experience God's power in our ministry.

The following Bible Study, **'The Power in Ministry'**, is a continuation of this section.

Bible Study: *The Power in Ministry*

T he testimonies in the book of Acts about the life of the first churches (e.g. the ministries of the apostles and the first Christians) tend to make us jealous. They make us ask: 'How did these simple people have such powerful and effective ministries?' In our church-life we can be heavily involved in all kinds of activities and yet see little fruit. Deep down in our hearts we realise that something is lacking, something which the Christians did have at that time. In this study we will discuss the secret of their ministry.

1. In Acts 4:13 the priests and religious leaders discover the secret of the apostles. Read this verse and fill in the blanks:

    By nature Peter and John were _____

    _____ ,

    but they spoke with boldness and had power to

    heal, because _____

    _____ .

2. The apostles had spent three years with Jesus, but this had not been just a simple acquaintance. During this period Jesus passed on His ministry to His disciples.

    Describe in your own words what Jesus means in John 14:12 and 20:21.

    _____

    _____

    _____

    _____

Personal Notes

3. It is the ministry of Jesus which is being continued through the Holy Spirit in the apostles and other Christians like Stephen for example (Acts 6:8). As Jesus was sent, so He sends us. Therefore we will first examine the ministry of Jesus.

Characteristics of the ministry of Jesus are shown in the Old Testament. In Isaiah 11:1–2 e.g. we see the first characteristics, i.e. the Spirit of:

_____

_____

_____

_____

Power is not just the only characteristic mentioned here, as power without wisdom is very dangerous! Read Luke 2:40 and 52. What was the *first characteristic* in the still young life of Jesus?

_____

4. In Isaiah 42:1–4 we find a *second characteristic* of the ministry of the Messiah.

Verse 1 speaks about what the Messiah will bring, i.e.:

_____

_____

The Hebrew word for *justice* is a broad concept and may also be translated *righteousness* and *right*.

Verse 2 speaks about the demeanour – the character – of the Messiah. Also look at Isaiah 53:11, and describe this in your own words:

_____

_____

_____

_____

This Person – humble and meek – is the One who will bring justice, righteousness, right.

This has been fulfilled in Jesus Christ. Read Romans 3:23–26 and 5:1. Summarise the second characteristic of His ministry:

_____

_____

_____

_____

What does this mean for us according to 2 Corinthians 5:18–6:10?

_____

_____

_____

_____

5.   The *third characteristic* we find in Isaiah 61:1–2. The Messiah came as the Anointed One. He was full of the Holy Spirit.

What Scripture passage does Jesus read in Luke 4:18–19?

_____

_____

What does Jesus comment on these verses in Luke 4:21b?

_____

_____

Personal Notes

Jesus lived and served by the power of the Holy Spirit. Read the following verses and write down what happened in relation to the Holy Spirit and the life of Jesus.

- Matthew 1:18; Luke 1:35 _____

  _____

- Luke 3:21–22 _____

  _____

- Luke 4:1 _____

  _____

- Luke 4:14, 15 _____

  _____

6. A *fourth characteristic* of the Messiah is found in Isaiah 9:6. The Messiah brings a new Kingdom of which He is the Prince of Peace.

    Read Luke 4:43. What did Jesus preach?

    _____

    _____

    Read Acts 1:1–3. After His resurrection Jesus spoke about:

    _____

    _____

    The Kingdom takes shape through proclamation. It has the following important features:

    a) It is *by* _____ (Luke 4:18)

    b) It is *for* _____ (Matthew 9:12)

    c) It is *against* _____ (John 12:31)

    d) It is *with* _____ of the Spirit
        (Hebrews 2:3–4)

7. Jesus said: *'As the Father has sent me, I am sending you.'* The first church knew the four characteristics of the ministry of Jesus.

   Mention them once more below:

   a) _____

   b) _____

   c) _____

   d) _____

8. If we want to grow in ministry these characteristics will have to be present. We should ask ourselves the following questions:

   a) Do I want to grow in wisdom and grace?

      ○ Yes

      ○ No

   b) Do I have a desire to be an ambassador for Christ, to proclaim the righteousness of God (2 Corinthians 5:18–21)?

      ○ Yes

      ○ No

      For Paul the consequences were suffering and persecution. Describe your own thoughts and feelings about these consequences. After writing them down bring them to God in prayer.

      _____

      _____

      _____

c) The ministry is by the Holy Spirit. Mark 'Yes' or 'No':

Are you born again by the Spirit?

○ Yes

○ No

Do you pray regularly to be filled with the Spirit?

○ Yes

○ No

Do you pray for the Spirit's guidance?

○ Yes

○ No

Is it your desire to serve in the power of the Spirit?

○ Yes

○ No

d) The main issue at stake is not that of building a church. God wants to reveal His Kingdom, of which the church is a servant. As the church preaches the Kingdom of which Jesus Christ is Lord (Acts 2:36), God will build His church (Acts 2:47b).

Is this viewpoint new to you?

_____

_____

_____

Is there anything in it that appeals to you?

_____

_____

_____

_____

Answers

1. unschooled and ordinary people; they had been with Jesus

2. Jesus is going to the Father and transfers His ministry as well as His authority to His disciples. As the Father sent Him (in His authority and power), Jesus sends His disciples.

3. The Spirit of wisdom and of understanding, of counsel and of power, of knowledge and of the fear of the Lord.

    Jesus was filled with wisdom.

4. Justice, righteousness, right.

    He will not achieve this by brute force, but through suffering He will overcome and reveal God's righteousness.

    Jesus died in our place for our sins, in order that we might be made righteous before God, that we might be enabled to live a righteous life, and that God's justice might be shown.

    To proclaim this message of reconciliation and righteousness even through suffering and persecution. We are ambassadors for Christ.

5. Isaiah 61:1–2

    'Today this Scripture is fulfilled in your hearing.' Jesus is the One anointed in the power of the Holy Spirit.

    - Jesus was born of the Holy Spirit.
    - Jesus was anointed for ministry after water baptism and the Holy Spirit coming upon Him.
    - Jesus was led by the Holy Spirit.
    - Jesus ministered in the power of the Holy Spirit.

6. The good news of the Kingdom.

    The Kingdom of God.

    a) the power of the Holy Spirit
    b) the sick, the needy, those in trouble
    c) satan
    d) the gifts

7. a) Filled with the Spirit of wisdom.
    b) Showing God's righteousness through suffering.
    c) Anointed.
    d) Preaching the Kingdom of God.

8. All questions: personal answers

SECTION 4
Spiritual Warfare

Introduction

S piritual warfare is a reality for everyone who is born again and has become a child of God. When we are born again we cross over from the kingdom of darkness into the Kingdom of Jesus Christ. This is what Paul states in Colossians 1:13:

'God, the Father, has rescued us from the dominion of darkness and brought us into the Kingdom of the Son He loves.'

The *defensive* part of our spiritual warfare is that we resist the attacks of satan in the power of God, and stand in the victory over satan that Christ has won for us.

In the natural we have satan, the devil, as our father and serve him (John 8:42–47). As soon as we come to God in repentance, and through the Holy Spirit receive new life, a fight will start. Satan will try anything at any time to lead us astray again. Especially when we become active in serving Jesus we can expect resistance and attacks. This fight takes place on different fronts:

- within us

- in the visible realm

- in the spiritual realm

In this study we will concentrate particularly on the struggle that takes place within us.

The *offensive* part of spiritual warfare is that as disciples of Jesus we have a commission from God to make disciples of all nations. The people in this world are under the power of satan (2 Corinthians 4:3–4) and cannot see the truth. Therefore we need to bring people the power of God for salvation. We need to live in the good of Jesus' victory, show this victory to the world and proclaim it (Colossians 2:15; Zechariah 4:6). This will enable God to use us to lead other people into this same place of victory.

With regard to our ministry it is absolutely essential that we are aware of spiritual warfare. Over and above that, we need to know our weapons for defence and attack, and how to use them.

Key Verses

2 Kings 6:15–18	Daniel 10:2–14
Ephesians 6:10–18	Revelation 12:7–17
2 Corinthians 4:4	Luke 11:14–26
1 Peter 5:5–9	Ephesians 1:17–23
James 4:7	Colossians 2:15

PART 4.1
The Kingdom of God

Jesus preached the Kingdom of God as His good news. In Mark's Gospel we find many parables regarding this Kingdom. Even after His resurrection Jesus taught His disciples about the Kingdom, which shows us how important it is. After His ascension, the apostles followed Jesus' example in this.

God's Kingdom manifests itself through the Holy Spirit (Matthew 12:28). It enters this dark world with power in order to save, to change, to heal and to deliver.

God wants to establish His Kingdom on earth (Matthew 6:10). In Jesus' ministry this is brought out time and again (e.g. Matthew 4:17, 23; 6:33). This is why Jesus came (Colossians 1:12–14). The Kingdom of God is not a matter of eating and drinking, but of righteousness, peace and joy in the Holy Spirit (Romans 14:17; 1 Corinthians 4:20). Jesus said:

'The Kingdom of God does not come with your careful observation, nor will people say, "Here it is," or "There it is," because the Kingdom of God is within you.'

(Luke 17:20, 21)

Wherever we go as ambassadors for Christ, there the Kingdom of God goes as well. Therefore our lives must demonstrate the righteousness, peace, joy and power of God. When we preach the good news it must go hand in hand with our deeds. The people around us should be able to notice the Kingdom of God in our lives, just like they did in the life of Jesus.

When will this Kingdom have fully come? Jesus said:

> *'And this gospel of the Kingdom will be preached in the whole world as a testimony to all nations, and then the end will come.'*
> (Matthew 24:14)

Jesus will return with power and great glory. Then He will establish a new heaven and a new earth where there will be justice. As disciples of Jesus we must be ready and well prepared for that day (2 Peter 3:10–14). That is the time the Kingdom will have fully come.

PART 4.2
Satan and His Kingdom

In the New Testament we see a world order that is the complete opposite of the government of God. This world order is under satan's rule (1 John 5:19) and has aims that are totally contrary to the aims of God's Kingdom.

This realm of satan has certain characteristics. It is a system that:

- always operates along the same lines

- is opposed to God as a whole

- resists the redeeming work of the Son

- hates Him (John 7:7)

- is ruled by the *'prince of this world'* (John 12:31)

- will pass away (Revelation 20:10)

We perceive the above mentioned characteristics of satan's realm through:

- our five senses

- contacts with other people in this world

- involvement in its circumstances and events

- the influence of current ideas

- the deception of society's norms and principles (or their absence)

- forms of government, politics, social stress, education etc.

In the natural man this finds its expression in the following ways:

- blindness, darkness (2 Corinthians 4:4)
- evil (Galatians 1:4; John 3:19)
- sin (Matthew 18:7)
- worries (Mark 4:19)
- ignorance of God (John 1:10)
- hopelessness (Ephesians 2:12)
- evil desires (2 Peter 1:4)
- pride, lust (1 John 2:16)
- deceit (2 John 7)
- evil powers (Ephesians 6:12; 1 Corinthians 2:6)

Spiritual warfare starts when we begin to recognise that we are involved in the conflict between light and darkness. In the power of God we have the authority to resist the powers of darkness. In this way the power of God is shown in the world. It is, however, up to us to be aware of powers rallying against us in this struggle and to learn how to overcome them.

PART 4.3
No Dualism

Nowhere in the Bible do we read that satan's power is in any respect equal to God's power. Some people believe in *dualism*, i.e. that there are two equal forces facing each other, and that the outcome of the fight is uncertain. However, this is not a battle between equals:

- satan is well-organised, yet not superior

- powerful, yet not all-powerful

- not tied to one place, yet not omnipresent

- intelligent, yet not all-knowing

Satan is an angel and not God. This means he is a creature and therefore subject to God. He once was a mighty angel, called Lucifer, one of the archangels. He fell from that position because of pride (Isaiah 14:12–15). There is a struggle, but satan is not equal to God. There is no reason therefore to be afraid of satan, as we are safe in Christ. However, if we step outside of our position in Christ we will be in danger.

It is a revolt of a creature, a created angel, against his Creator, the Almighty. The outcome of this struggle is already decided. Jesus Christ has broken the power of satan and has disarmed him (Colossians 2:15). The reason believers have the impression that this is a fight between equals is due to the fact that they do not know the great and sovereign God. If we do not know God and His power in a deep personal sense, then satan's power seems to be very great indeed. Jesus was aware of His authority in God and the demons had to flee (Mark 1:21–28). See also Daniel 11:32.

PART 4.4
Man's Position

God created man in His own image and gave him authority to rule over all the earth and to subdue it (Genesis 1:26–28; Psalm 8:3–8).

God's intention was that man should rule over the earth. Through the Fall man gave up his control over the world to satan (1 John 5:19).

As believers we have been raised with Christ. God put everything under Christ's feet. In Christ, therefore, we who are believers have regained our authority. In the name of Jesus we have authority over all the works of the devil.

When Jesus returned to the Father after His victory over satan, He asked the Father to give the Holy Spirit to all who believe in Him. Satan will come up against us as believers, but in Christ we are more than conquerors (Romans 8:37). This means that the same power which Jesus had is available to us now and that in His Name we are given the same authority.

By giving us His authority Jesus shares His victory with His followers.

> '*The reason the Son of God appeared was to destroy the devil's work.*'   (1 John 3:8)

PART 4.5
Our Strategy in Spiritual Warfare

F irst of all we need to ask for insight and wisdom for each particular situation. Too often negative events are put down to the work of satan, when this may not necessarily be the case. We should first try to find out who, or what, is actually the cause. The following possibilities should be considered:

i) Our old self

Many battles are the result of our own sins. Sometimes Christians think that they are under attack from satan, when in actual fact they should repent of their sins (Isaiah 30:15; 59:1, 2; James 1:13–15).

ii) Satan's doing

When we know that we are under attack from the enemy we need to do the following:

- size up his tricks (2 Corinthians 2:10, 11)

- humble ourselves and submit to God (James 4:7a)

- resist the devil and give him no chance to get any further (James 4:7; Ephesians 4:27)

- recognise where God is at work and act according to His will in that particular situation

iii) God's doing

In the book of Job we see that God allows satan a limited amount of room (Job 1:6–12). Job recognised this and was able to persevere in his struggle (Job 1:20–22) Through this struggle Job came to know God at a deeper level (Job 42:5). See also Romans 8:28, 31–39.

PART 4.6
Our Spiritual Armour

i) Weapons for defence

To be able to stand our ground with the enemy we need to put on the full armour of God (Ephesians 6:10–18). First of all we need to be aware of the fact that it is God's armour, not ours. Only the things that God supplies are going to give us the protection needed.

All parts of the armour together constitute Christ Himself. When we remain in Christ we share in His victory. That is why we have to put on Christ (Galatians 3:27) and remain in Him.

The armour of God is divided into a number of items. The best way to look at the different weapons is to regard them as a protection against any point where the enemy can come and attack us. By doing so we will discover the best way to resist the attacks of the enemy.

For each part of the armour we will discuss the following points:

- Which attack of the enemy does it protect us against?

- What is the significance of each weapon?

- What is our personal responsibility when wielding each weapon?

a) The belt of truth

Satan attacks us with lies and deception. He has done so from the beginning, starting with Adam and Eve (Genesis 3). Jesus calls him the father of lies (John 8:44). Satan always tries to make us doubt the Word of God. From the start he has distorted the Word of God and misquoted it. That is why many Christians despair about themselves, because we so often believe what the enemy says about us than what God says. We often do not even have a clear picture of God Himself.

The weapon against this attack is *'the belt of truth'*. The truth will expose the lie about God or our position in Christ and overcome it. The truth will set us free (John 8:30–32).

⇨   Our own personal responsibility here is to put on the *'belt of truth'*. This implies:

- studying the truth

- believing the truth

- obeying the truth

- speaking the truth

- proclaiming the truth

b) The breastplate of righteousness

When satan cannot pierce our armour with lies he will try to do so with evil, sinful desires. This usually starts in our minds, and may contaminate our motives, which will have their influence on our will.

The weapon against this attack is God's righteousness. We cannot resist satan by our own goodness or moral standards. We are justified in Christ and received His righteousness as a breastplate or robe. This enables us to live a righteous and pure life according to God's norms.

⇨   Our personal responsibility is:

- to accept God's righteousness

- to believe that we have been justified in Christ

- to reject impurity and sinful desires

c) Readiness to proclaim the gospel of peace

Satan can allure us into living an easy life. If he cannot make us confused, he will try and make it as quiet and sociable as possible for us, so that we do not make him confused. Many Christians are discouraged in evangelism and are now leading a quiet Christian life. However, we must not give up the Great Commission (Matthew 28:18–20).

The weapon against this attack is God's promise: *'I am with you'* (Matthew 28:20). God blesses those who bear witness to Him. This does not mean that we will have no problems, on the contrary it often means persecution and suffering.

⇨ Our personal responsibility is:

- to be prepared to preach the gospel every-where

d) The shield of faith

The devil attacks us by way of unbelief. When there is unbelief he is given the opportunity to shoot *'flaming arrows'* at us and hurt us. We are well aware of the doubts that surprise us at times, and the fear of failure that so often cripples us. 'Does God truly hear me?' Unbelief is paralysing.

However, God has given us a weapon: *'the shield of faith'*. Faith rests securely on God's promises. Between us and the *'flaming arrows'* we lift the shield of faith in Christ. That kind of faith is an impenetrable weapon.

⇨ Here our personal responsibility is:

- to throw off all hindrances and sin (Hebrews 12:1, 2)

- to open ourselves to the gift of faith

- to stand on the rich promises of God

e) The helmet of salvation

The enemy attacks us through catastrophes and accidents.

The word *salvation* (redemption) in the New Testament means both physical and spiritual well-being. Jesus said about satan: *'he is a murderer from the beginning'* (John 8:44). Satan not only aims his attack at the assurance of our salvation in Christ, but also at our bodies or circumstances. Of course there are instances where God allows a violent death (e.g. Stephen), but here God was in charge of that life and Stephen was certain of his salvation in Christ.

The weapon against this attack is: *'the helmet of salvation'*. We may know for sure that we are God's children. The blood of Jesus has redeemed us, gives us salvation and blessing, and God's protection besides. Jesus is the author of our salvation (Hebrews 2:10).

⇨ Our personal responsibility is:

- to ask God for protection

- to believe that there is power in the blood of Jesus

- to follow the author of our faith, Jesus Christ the Lord

f) The sword of the Spirit

We often lack the balance between Word and Spirit. This makes it easy for satan to attack us. The Spirit operates through the Word and the Word becomes alive through the Spirit. Without this balance we are powerless.

The sword of the Spirit is the Word of God. This is a weapon for defence as well as for attack. In Matthew 4:1–11 we find an example of this, where Jesus used the Word against satan's temptations. We too may use the Word of God in this way.

⇨ Our personal responsibility is:

- to know the Word of God

- to apply the Word; **wield** it in battle

- to proclaim the Word in the power of the Holy Spirit

g) Praying in the Spirit

Neglecting our prayer life weakens our faith relationship with God. This makes us an easy target for satan.

Paul calls us to pray without ceasing. This helps us to stay tuned in to God and remain under His protection. To pray without ceasing does not mean living in seclusion all the time. Here it means maintaining a natural prayer relationship with our Heavenly Father, even when we are at work.

Through praying in the Spirit we will perceive God's leading and His will. This will result in answered prayers.

⇨ It is our personal responsibility:

- to **speak** with the Father continuously

- to persevere in prayer

- to be sensitive to the Holy Spirit's leading

ii) Weapons for attack

When satan has got a grip on someone's life, or when he wants to frustrate us as disciples of Jesus, then we not only have authority in God to defend ourselves, but also to attack him. In these attacks we have at our disposal:

a) The Name of Jesus

In the New Testament the name of Jesus is most important. In Colossians 3:17 Paul says:

> *'And whatever you do, whether in word or deed, do it all in the name of the Lord Jesus...'*

What is the significance of the name of Jesus? Throughout the Bible names have great significance, as a name refers to the whole person, his character, personality and authority. There are people who through the name of Jesus have become believers. Others receive the Holy Spirit, some are healed and yet others are set free from satan's power. When using the name of Jesus we acknowledge the fact that we are not trying to help or counsel people in our own name. We do it as representatives of Jesus.

The name of Jesus is a powerful weapon in our hands. We must always mention it with reverence. This is the name at which one day every knee will bow and which every tongue will confess (Philippians 2:9–10).

b) The Word of God

In Ephesians 6:17 the Word of God is described as *'the sword of the Spirit'*. It is a weapon for attack, but may be used for defence as well. The Word is living and active when it is being proclaimed in the power of the Holy Spirit. No combination is more powerful than the Spirit and the Word of God. When these two go hand in hand, in balance, one may be sure of exposing the enemy and putting him to flight.

c) The power of the Holy Spirit

Jesus was anointed with the power of the Holy Spirit; by this the Kingdom of God forged ahead (Matthew 12:28; Acts 10:38). This is true for us as well. Through the functioning of the gifts of the Holy Spirit we will also be able to discern whether something is *from above* or *from below*: i.e. 'Is it from God?' 'Is it just human nature?' or 'Is it from satan?' The gifts of the Spirit will be dealt with more extensively in Sections 5–8.

PART 4.7
How to Grow in Leading a Victorious Christian Life

S piritual warfare is a daily ingredient of the circumstances in which we live. We still live in occupied territory, so how can we learn to lead a constant life of victory over the enemy? Below are a few practical tips:

- *Know and live in Jesus' authority*. We have been redeemed out of satan's hand. We stand in the total victory of Jesus (Revelation 12:11).

- *Be constantly filled with the Holy Spirit* and *walk in the Spirit*, not after the lusts of the flesh (Galatians 5:16; Ephesians 5:18).

- *Stay away from occult practices*. If you have already dabbled in these, then renounce them and ask God to forgive you for each thing you have done that has dishonoured God.

- *Keep the sinful nature crucified with Christ* (Galatians 2:20). This we do by having faith in Christ.

- *Wear a garment of praise* (Isaiah 61:3); be joyful always; pray continually; give thanks in all circumstances (1 Thessalonians 5:16–18).

- *Fellowship with other Christians regularly* (Hebrews 10:25).

- *Cut any association with those who would draw you back into sinful or occult activities* (2 Thessalonians 3:6; 1 Corinthians 5:9; Ephesians 5:11).

- *Actively resist satan and whatever he tries to get you to do*, i.e. reject his influence (James 4:7; Colossians 3:8). This is particularly true for your mind.

- *Wear the whole armour of God* (Ephesians 6:10–18).

- *Live in freedom*. Your salvation and redemption are complete (2 Corinthians 3:17).

- *Be clear in your communication*.

- *Deal with frustrations*.

SECTION 5
The Gifts of Grace

Introduction

Key Verses

Introduction

In Sections 5–8 a distinction is made between:

- talents
- gifts
- ministries

By *talents* we mean our natural abilities, which we may use in the church after they have been sanctified by and consecrated to God.

Gifts are the abilities that are freely given to us by the Holy Spirit. These give us authority the moment we start using the gift.

Ministries are given by the Spirit as well; they give us continuous authority, for as long as we have a particular ministry.

Key Verses

1 Peter 4:10

Romans 11:29

John 14:12–27

PART 5.1
The Giver: the Holy Spirit

The Holy Spirit is not a vague influence or mystic idea, *He is a person*. He is the third member of the threefold Godhead.

Like God the Father and God the Son, the Holy Spirit is:

* eternal (Hebrews 9:14)

* present everywhere (Psalm 139:7)

* all knowing (1 Corinthians 2:9–10)

* all powerful (Luke 1:35)

He shows personal attributes:

* intellect (Romans 8:27)

* will (1 Corinthians 12:11)

* sensitivity (Ephesians 4:30)

He is right inside our life situations, communicating with us, opening Himself up to us and looking for us to open up ourselves to Him in response.

Without the Holy Spirit we could never know God's strength in our daily lives or ministries. The life and power of Jesus Christ will be manifested in and through our lives by the Holy Spirit.

PART 5.2
The Holy Spirit and the Church

God's purpose, the Church, is revealed through the Holy Spirit. After the outpouring of the Holy Spirit in Acts 2 we see the development and growth of the Church. The following are characteristics of a church that was quickened and led by the Holy Spirit, as mentioned in Acts 2:41–47:

- about three thousand repented and were baptised

- they were being taught by the apostles

- they had fellowship, they cared about one another

- they celebrated the Lord's Supper; the sacrifice of Jesus was in the centre

- there were wonders and miraculous signs

- they had everything in common

- some sold their possessions, and gave to the poor as they had need

- they held regular and frequent meetings

- they were glad and they praised God

- they enjoyed the favour of all the people

- the Lord added to their number daily

In the history of the Church the fire of the Holy Spirit has been quenched many times, but when the Church begins to pray for a fresh outpouring of the Holy Spirit, the Lord will revive His Church. During such a revival these characteristics will be evident again.

Because of the power and the renewing work of the Holy Spirit the true Church of Christ exists and is growing worldwide, even today! The gifts of the Spirit are given for the specific purpose of edifying the whole Church (1 Corinthians 12–14).

PART 5.3
Ask and You Will Receive

I t is the work of the Holy Spirit to make us *thirst for God* in our hearts (Psalm 42:1, 2). This causes us to long for the Holy Spirit. God invites us to come to Him (Isaiah 55:1; John 7:37–39).

God gives His Spirit that we might glorify Him. We glorify God *by obeying Him in love*. That is why obedience must be the attitude of our hearts (Acts 5:32).

The Holy Spirit makes us aware of our need of His power in our lives. If you know you need Him in your life, why do you not *ask the Father* to fill you with His Holy Spirit. Do not be afraid of what God might do.

> *'God has not given us a Spirit of fear, but of power and of love and a sound mind.'*   (2 Timothy 1:7)

Open yourself to God, let the wind of the Holy Spirit blow through you. If you are looking to God, He will not give you something that is bad or evil (Luke 11:9–13).

Focus your attention on Jesus and on your heavenly Father, then be open to receive all that they give you. Let the Holy Spirit sanctify you through and through: spirit, soul and body (1 Thessalonians 5:23). Let Him fill your life with God's power. Receive from Him the gifts He brings and learn how to praise, worship and witness in the power of God.

If you want to be filled with the Holy Spirit you can pray:

- either on your own,

- or with someone who knows what it means to be filled with the Holy Spirit

Personal Notes

Sometimes it is easier to pray with someone who knows what it means (Acts 8:14–17; 19:6). Use a simple prayer such as under Part 5.4. Your heavenly Father will hear you and answer you and you will be filled with the Holy Spirit.

What matters most is not that you have an experience, but that you have *faith in the promise of the Father*.

PART 5.4
A Simple Prayer

It is essential to our life and service that we are continuously filled with the Holy Spirit. Therefore, we should seek to be filled with the Holy Spirit daily.

Be honest and open to God. If you are aware of any particular sins, confess them, mentioning them specifically. The following prayer is an example:

> 'Heavenly Father, thank You for the promise that whoever asks will receive, and whoever seeks will find. I know that I need more of Your power in my life. Father I confess my sin before You, I forgive all those who wronged me, and ask You for Your cleansing in my life through the blood of Jesus. I open my life completely to You. Please fill me now with the power of Your Holy Spirit. I thank You for this because You promised it. In Jesus' name. Amen.'

PART 5.5
The Grace of God

None of us deserves God's love, but He has shown it to us, and bestowed it on us in Christ. Grace is exactly that: receiving an undeserved gift. Grace is the foundation of our lives and our service for God (Romans 12:3).

C. Peter Wagner, in *Your Spiritual Gifts Can Help Your Church Grow*, has defined a spiritual gift as follows:

> 'A spiritual gift is an extraordinary ability given by the Holy Spirit to each member of the Body of Christ – according to God's grace – to be used within the Body of Christ.'

This definition clearly shows the relationship between spiritual gifts and the grace of God.

In the New Testament there is a close relationship between the words *gift* and *grace*. In fact both words have the same root. The Greek word for gift is **charisma** whereas the word for grace is **charis**. The ending of the word **charisma** may be translated *the result of*. The so-called spiritual gift then is *the result of grace*. In other words, a gift is the expression or outworking of God's grace (1 Peter 4:10).

When we are in the Father's service we are enabled to do this through the gifts of the Spirit which are available to us by grace. So by way of our work the grace of God becomes available to others. Paul experienced this and said:

> 'But by the grace of God I am what I am, and his grace to me was not without effect. No, I worked harder than all of them – yet not I, but the grace of God that was with me.'   (1 Corinthians 15:10)

SECTION 6
The Gifts of the Holy Spirit

Introduction

T he gifts of the Holy Spirit are God's power in action. They will become manifest in our lives when we find ourselves in circumstances where their working is very much needed. It is not in our own strength that we carry out our spiritual ministry, but God will reveal Himself in the situation by equipping us with the gifts of the Holy Spirit. This will lift us beyond the limits of our own weaknesses, constraints or talents. Through the gifts of the Holy Spirit we are equipped to execute His will.

Without the gifts we live and function at the level of our natural abilities, talents and strength. With the gifts of the Spirit we function at the level of God's ability, insight and potentialities. The well-known author A.W. Tozer put it like this:

> 'Religious work may be carried out by ordinary, "natural" people who do not have the gifts of the Holy Spirit. They may do it well and with competence, but work destined for eternity can only be done by the Eternal Spirit of God. No work has eternal value unless it is brought about by the Holy Spirit through the gifts He Himself puts into the souls of redeemed people.'

As Christians we may ask God to give us His gifts in particular situations. If we ask for them from a pure heart and with the right motivation, the Father will supply us with the gifts that are needed. In this way we will discover that God wants to use us through His gifts.

'Now to each one the manifestation of the Spirit is given for the common good.' (1 Corinthians 12:7)

Key Verses

1 Corinthians 12:1–11

Romans 12:4–8

1 Corinthians 12:12–27

PART 6.1
Gifts of the Trinity

In 1 Corinthians 12 Paul makes clear to us the tremendous fact that there is unity between the Father, the Son and the Holy Spirit in the operating of the gifts of the Holy Spirit. In fact, we should not just speak about the gifts of the Spirit, but rather about the gifts of the Father, the Son and the Holy Spirit.

In verses 4–6 Paul uses three different expressions that complement each other:

i)   'Different kinds of gifts, but the same *Spirit*'

This points us to the source of the gifts. The Holy Spirit is the bearer of these gifts. They are mentioned in:

- **Romans 12:4–8**
  The gifts mentioned here are connected with someone's personality and serve to equip a person for a specific task within the church; e.g. someone could be given the gift of leadership, someone else the gift of mercy. Therefore we can call them ***personality gifts***.

- **1 Corinthians 12:7–11**

  These gifts of the Holy Spirit are gifts of, as well as gifts for, the whole Body of Christ. They find their expression and use within the local church of Christ. These gifts are given spontaneously, e.g. during meetings, evangelistic activities or counselling sessions. It appears that Body gifts are available to everyone who asks God for them, and in general will suit the needs of the church at that particular point in time. Therefore they are called *Body gifts*.

ii) 'Different kinds of service, but the same *Lord'*

This talks about different ministries, or tasks. These ministries are mentioned in Ephesians 4:7–16. In the life of Jesus we see these five ministries combined. It is essential that all these ministries find their expression within the leadership of the church.

iii) 'Different kinds of working, but the same *God works all of them in all men'*

In the Greek the word used here for *works* is *energemata*. It includes the word *energy*. From the Father, through the Son, and by the power of the Holy Spirit God's redeeming and renewing power is being released into this world. In this way the Kingdom of God is manifested through the Church.

This work of the Father, Son and Holy Spirit may be summarised as follows:

The Father

> 'God the Father who works all of them in all men.'
> (1 Corinthians 12:6)

The Son

- *Gifts of service* (Ephesians 4:7–16): apostles, prophets, evangelists, pastors and teachers

> 'To prepare God's people for works of service, so that the body of Christ may be built up.'
> (Ephesians 4:13)

The Holy Spirit

- *Personality gifts* (Romans 12:3–8): prophesying, serving, teaching, encouraging, giving, leadership, showing mercy etc.

- *Body gifts* (1 Corinthians 12:7–11): message of wisdom, message of knowledge, faith, healing, miraculous powers, prophecy, distinguishing between spirits, tongues, interpretation of tongues

Therefore, it is not so much our practising the gifts of the Holy Spirit, as the triune God involving us in His dynamic work in the church by His gifts!

Remarks: Although the gifts have been divided into different groups, in practice, they work together. When we use our personality gifts or ministry within the church we need the Body gifts as well.

PART 6.2
Body Gifts

In 1 Corinthians 12:8–10 nine of them are mentioned:

i) Wisdom (the message of wisdom)

Definition

The God-given ability to search for God's truth and make it applicable to life; by divine revelation, to be able to pass on the purposes and thoughts of God as an aid to solving a particular situation.

Examples

- Solomon (1 Kings 3:24–28)
- Jesus (John 8:4–7)

Wisdom is the basis for our service from which we may reach out to others. Without the gift of God's wisdom we will make a lot of mistakes, make wrong decisions, take hasty steps and probably leave a trail of insecurity and hurt. Wisdom is the ability to see things the way God sees them; to discern the heart of the matter so that we may know what is best, and what to do in a specific situation. Here we have to remember that the message of wisdom is not primarily a specific word to be passed on to others. Rather, it is a God-given word meant for someone trying to help somebody else, in order to provide the insight and wisdom needed to meet that person's need.

ii) Knowledge (the message of knowledge)

Definition

The God-given ability to know the truth through the inspiration of the Holy Spirit; to know, by divine revelation, certain facts about someone's life or a specific situation.

Examples

- Joseph (Genesis 41:25–32)

- Elisha (2 Kings 6:8–12)

- Jesus (John 4:17–18; Matthew 21:2–3)

Knowledge, like wisdom, is also is a gift of insight, but a word of knowledge is a revelation to be shared with the person involved.

A word of knowledge often contains elements which reveal a still hidden problem (or sin) and thereby produce far more room for the Holy Spirit than before.

The gifts of wisdom and knowledge often co-operate, as the first one enables the application of the second one (Luke 20:20–26).

iii) Faith (power of faith)

Definition

The God-given ability to trust God for the improbable and to stimulate other people's vision; a divine enabling to have faith, and be absolutely certain that God will reveal His power in a given situation.

Examples

- Joshua (Joshua 10:12–14)

- Elijah (1 Kings 18:17–40)

- Jesus (Mark 4:37–40; John 11:41–44)

Faith is the gift that provides assurance and confidence in a time of ministry. Through the gift of faith we are certain of what God is going to do and we are given the power to believe that this will surely happen.

iv) Gifts of healings

Definition

The God-given ability to administer to a person the life of Jesus for spiritual, emotional and physical healing; a divine enabling to administer God's healing power.

Examples

- Jesus (Mark 1:29–31; 3:1–5)

- Philip (Acts 8:6–7)

- Paul (Acts 14:9–10)

The words *gifts* and *healings* are both plural, because there are so many gifts of healing relating to the many different illnesses and hurts from which people suffer.

v) Miraculous powers (signs and wonders)

Definition

The God-given ability to perform miracles that defy the laws of nature, through superhuman power; a divine enabling to do supernatural deeds.

Examples

- Elisha (2 Kings 4:1–7)

- Jesus (John 2:1–11; Luke 9:16–17)

- Stephen (Acts 6:8)

A miracle is something that surpasses the process of natural laws. The things that happen can only be attributed to a direct intervention by God and thereby reveal the tremendous power of God; e.g. raising of the dead, changing water to wine, etc.

vi) Prophecy (inspired speech)

Definition

The gift of prophecy is the God-given ability to receive and pass on direct messages from God.

Examples

- Zechariah (Luke 1:67)

- Simeon (Luke 2:25–35)

- Jesus (Matthew 24:3–42; John 21:18)

Prophecy is given for the edification of the Church. It is very direct and requires a response. Paul calls the Church to eagerly desire this gift in particular (1 Corinthians 14:1–6; 22–23, 39–40).

vii) Distinguishing between spirits

Definition

The God-given ability to distinguish between truth and falsehood and between good and evil; to receive insight by divine revelation, in order to know what kind of spirit is present in a person or a situation.

Examples

- John the Baptist (Matthew 12:34)

- Jesus (Luke 13:11–16; John 8:44)

- Paul (Acts 13:6–12; 16:16–18)

The Bible says that we should test the spirits to see whether they are from God (1 John 4:1). It is by this gift of discernment that we are best able to know which kind of spirit we are up against in a given situation.

viii) Different kinds of tongues

Definition

The God-given ability to speak in a language of men or angels that has not been learned by the speaker beforehand.

Examples

- Apostles (Acts 2:4)

- Believers at the house of Cornelius (Acts 10:46; Mark 16:17)

- Paul (1 Corinthians 14:18)

> *'For anyone who speaks in a tongue does not speak to men but to God. Indeed, no-one understands him; he utters mysteries with his spirit ... He who speaks in a tongue edifies himself.'*
>
> (1 Corinthians 14:2, 4)

In 1 Corinthians 14 Paul explains a bit more about how to use the gift of tongues. Here two ways of using this gift are made clear:

a) For personal use. Speaking in a tongue builds one up, e.g. in one's quiet time. Personal use of speaking in tongues makes us more open to the Word of God. When we speak in tongues in our spirit we become sensitive to the will of God and His Word.

b) To pass on a message in the church. In this case it is important that the message is translated, and that the church is edified (1 Corinthians 14:26–28).

ix) Interpretation of tongues

Definition

The God-given ability to interpret the meaning of a tongue, without the interpreter having learned the language before-hand; the ability to interpret the contents of an unknown tongue in an intelligible language.

Example

- Church in Corinth (1 Corinthians 14:26–28)

This gift is appropriate in a meeting where the Spirit is responding to the exercise of the gift of tongues. What emerges is the dynamic quality of what has been said in a tongue. It is not a translation however, it is more like an interpretation or rendering. It could be defined a response. The Spirit uses a tongue to draw attention to the fact that God wants to say something, and this increases the level of expectation. The interpretation passes on the word of God, so that everybody is able to understand and to judge, and to act accordingly.

In order to be effective the different gifts of the Spirit often work together. The gift of healing, for example, may co-operate with the gifts of faith and discernment to produce the desired effect. In the same way the gift of faith may need the gifts of wisdom and discernment.

These **Body gifts** are not restricted to one person. The Holy Spirit will provide us with the necessary gifts at the right time so that God's purpose is brought about (1 Corinthians 12:11).

Personal Notes

PART 6.3
Personality Gifts

Apart from the Body gifts mentioned in 1 Corinthians 12 we have the *personality gifts* mentioned in Romans 12:4–8. These are closely connected with our personality.

i) Prophecy

Definition

The ability to regularly bring the prophetic word from the heart of God to the body of Christ.

Examples

- Ezckiel (Ezekiel 14)
- Peter (Acts 2:14–40)
- Peter (Acts 5:1–6)

God wants to share His heart with us. This could be a word for the whole church, or for us personally. In such a case it is important that we fully understand a situation. The words being shared might be words given to us directly by the Holy Spirit, or could be the interpretation of a word from Scripture appropriate to that particular situation.

ii) Serving

Definition

The ability to render help in such a way that it strengthens and encourages others.

Examples

- Jesus (John 13:1–16)
- Dorcas (Acts 9:36)
- Stephen (Acts 6:1–7)

A person having the gift of serving has the ability to identify with the needs in the church. Someone with this gift might also enable somebody else in the ministry.

iii) Teaching

Definition

The ability to study and interpret God's Word; and to be able to pass this on to others in a clear and systematic way.

Examples

- Jesus (Matthew 5:1–11)

- Apollos (Acts 18:24–28)

- Paul (2 Timothy 1:11)

People with this gift have the God-given ability to make people understand what God is saying and what His purpose is.

iv) Encouraging (exhorting, comforting)

Definition

The ability to motivate people, in order to enable them to function effectively; usually with the assistance of God's Word.

Example

- Paul and Barnabas (Acts 14:20–22)

This is a pastoral gift, given by God to share words of encouragement, comfort, correction and advice with church members, to help and heal them.

v) Contributing (to the needs of others)

Definition

The ability to collect money and to distribute it for the extension of the Kingdom of God. This should be done generously and open-handedly.

Examples

- The church in Macedonia (2 Corinthians 8:1–5)

- Barnabas (Acts 4:36–37)

The Bible promises rich blessings for the cheerful giver (Proverbs 11:25; 2 Corinthians 9:6–8).

vi) Leadership (governing)

Definition

The ability to lead others and to look after church matters. This should be done diligently and industriously.

Examples

- Joseph (Acts 7:9, 10)

- Elders (1 Timothy 5:17)

- Deacons (1 Timothy 3:12)

Leadership is a gift to set goals in accordance with God's plans for the future; to pass these on to other people in such a way that they willingly and harmoniously work together to achieve them.

vii) Showing mercy

Definition

The ability to reach out and comfort those who are often ignored by other people, or for whom others have no time. This will be done cheerfully and joyfully.

Examples

- The Samaritan (Luke 10:25–37)

- Jesus (Matthew 8:1–4; John 8:8–11)

- Barnabas (Acts 9:26–27)

- In Philippi (Acts 16:33, 34)

Showing mercy is one of the principles of the Kingdom of God. We should feel genuine compassion for those who suffer physically, spiritually or emotionally – Christians and non-Christians alike. When this compassion is translated into cheerful action, it will reveal the love and mercy of Christ and relieve the suffering.

Within the church these personality gifts may find their expression in tasks such as:

- prayer

- children's work

- praise and worship

- organisation

- practical work

Personal Notes

PART 6.4
The Ministry Gifts in Ephesians 4:11

In Ephesians 4:7 and 8 Paul says:

> '*But to each one of us **grace has been given** as Christ apportioned it. This is why it says: "When he ascended on high, he led captives in his train and **gave gifts to men**."*'

In Greek the word ***domata*** is used here for *gifts*. This in contrast with Romans 12 and 1 Corinthians 12 where the Greek text reads ***charisma***. The noun ***doma*** means *that which has been given* (to someone). The word implies that what has been given is something concrete. The emphasis is on the gift. In Ephesians 4:11 Paul mentions the five ministries that together make up the ministry (the gift) of Jesus:

i)   Apostles

Definition

An apostle is appointed by God to take on and execute the overall leadership over a number of churches. The churches recognise and acknowledge the apostle's exceptional authority in spiritual matters.

Examples

- Paul (2 Corinthians 12:11–12; Galatians 1:1)

- Peter and others (Acts 5:12–16; 15:1–2)

The word *apostle* is derived from a Greek word ***apostolos*** and literally means *sent one*. In the first instance it was the twelve that were the apostles, but Paul counts himself among them as well (1 Corinthians 15:7–9). The distinguishing mark of the first apostles was that they had met Jesus personally and could give evidence of His resurrection (Acts 1:21–26).

Since the twelve, others have been called apostles as well (Acts 4:3–4; Romans 16:7; Galatians 1:19). This ministry of apostleship did not die out with the first twelve (or else this ministry would not have been given to the first church). The preparation of believers has not been finished yet, and apostles are still needed for this even today.

ii) Prophets

Definition

The ability to convey a special message from God; passing on a word from God relating to a particular situation (sometimes relating to something in the future).

Examples

- Judas and Silas (Acts 15:32)
- Philip's daughters (Acts 21:9)
- Agabus (Acts 9:10, 11)

Characteristic of the ministry of prophets is that the Holy Spirit speaks through them to the church. We are not talking here about the spontaneous gift of prophecy (1 Corinthians 12:10) but about the ministry of a prophet. Through their preaching they encourage, exhort and edify the church. Together with the apostles, Paul, in his letter to the Ephesians, calls them the foundation of the church (Ephesians 2:20).

iii) Evangelists

Definition

The ministry of an evangelist is the God-given gift to share the gospel of Jesus with other people in such a way, that they become disciples and responsible members of the church.

Examples

- Timothy (2 Timothy 4:5)

- Philip (Acts 21:8; 8:4–13, 26–40)

The evangelist has the task of passing on the gospel in the widest sense of the word (2 Timothy 2:14, 15; 4:2). In the New Testament we read that they used to work in various churches as travelling evangelists.

iv) Pastors

Definition

A pastor has the God-given ability to look after the spiritual well-being of the church for a long period of time.

Examples

- Jesus (John 10:1–18)

- Elders (1 Peter 5:1–4)

In 1 Peter 5:2 the task of an elder is mentioned: watch over the flock. This means to look after the flock by protecting, feeding and caring for it. This pastoral ministry should not be carried out just because one feels obliged to do it (forced, reluctantly), but in accordance with God's will, i.e. willingly and wholeheartedly.

v) Teachers

Definition

This ministry is the God-given ability to teach people the right doctrine and conduct; so that believers will grasp God's Word and purpose.

Examples

- Jesus (Matthew 7:29)

- In Antioch (Acts 13:1)

- Paul (1 Timothy 2:7)

If people are to grow in their faith they need to be instructed in the truth; therefore teaching is a very important ministry. Paul warns that in later times some will abandon the faith because of false teaching (1 Timothy 4). Peter also gives a similar warning in 2 Peter 2.

Summary

1. The gifts and ministries are of the Holy Spirit. We therefore need to know and be filled with the Holy Spirit.

2. It is by God's grace only that we receive the Holy Spirit.

3. It is not for our personal benefit that spiritual gifts are given, but to enable us to serve the Body of Christ and to build it up.

4. The gifts of the Holy Spirit enable us to serve God with more than just our own potential, our own talents, because we reach out to others in the power of God.

5. The gifts of the Holy Spirit may be described as gifts of the Father, the Son and the Holy Spirit. It is God the Father who works it all out, it flows from His Father's heart; and it is the ministry of the Son, by the power of the Holy Spirit.

SECTION 7
Practising the Gifts

Introduction

T hese days much is being written and discussed about discovering one's gifts. The 'How-to-discover-your-gift' test is rather popular, but the discovering process is not so simple. There is no short road to exercising God's gifts. For that reason we started this study with sections on *love*, *brokenness*, *holiness*, *baptism with fire* and *spiritual warfare*.

As we look at discovering and practising the gifts we will continue to make a distinction between *Body gifts* (1 Corinthians 12), *personality gifts* (Romans 12) and *ministries* (Ephesians 4).

Key Verses

Psalm 37:1–11	Proverbs 10:22
Joel 2:28–30	Zechariah 4:6
Matthew 11:28–30	2 Corinthians 3:1–6
1 Corinthians 12:31; 14:1	2 Timothy 1:6

PART 7.1
The Body of Christ

W e must be clear about our motivation as we seek our gifts. It could be that we have spent a lot of time looking for gifts, but have not received them because we are looking for them from the wrong motives (James 4:1–3).

Gifts are given for the benefit of God and His Kingdom, not for our own benefit. The Body of Christ – the Church – is the servant of the Kingdom; that is why gifts and ministries are given for the whole Body and for the edification of the Church. In 1 Corinthians 12:12–27 Paul expounds this principle of the body.

What are the important features of the gifts?

- They are manifestations of the Spirit (1 Corinthians 12:7)

- They are the work of the Spirit (1 Corinthians 12:11)

- The Spirit gives them as He determines (1 Corinthians 12:11)

- They are given for the common good (1 Corinthians 12:7)

- Love is the avenue by which they are given (1 Corinthians 12:31–13:10)

- By using the gifts we edify ourselves (1 Corinthians 14:4)

- By using the gifts the church is being edified (1 Corinthians 14:4)

- They serve to prepare for works of service (Ephesians 4:12)

- They serve to build up the Body of Christ (Ephesians 4:12)

- They help the Body attain the fullness of Christ (Ephesians 4:13)

- They bring about growth of the Body (Ephesians 4:16)

- They build us up together in love (Ephesians 4:16)

PART 7.2
Four Conditions

If the four conditions mentioned below are not present in your life it will be very difficult to discover your gifts, let alone practise them.

i)   You must be a born again Christian

Many people attend church regularly but have no personal relationship with Jesus and have never experienced *new birth*, or what others might call *renewal/conversion*, or *decision for Christ*. What matters is not what you call it, but whether you have a personal relationship with Christ.

ii)   You need to be filled with the Holy Spirit

It is only by being baptised in or filled with the Holy Spirit that we can receive the gifts of the Holy Spirit. For this it is essential that we seek to live pure and holy lives that are surrendered to Jesus, and pray for the filling with the Holy Spirit. This is, and always will be, the foundation for a fruit-bearing ministry.

iii)   You must believe that the gifts of the Holy Spirit are also intended for you

Many Christians have no idea that God wants to equip them with the gifts of the Spirit. This may be due to:

a) Lack of teaching

Many people have never been taught about the gifts of the Holy Spirit and therefore know little about them. Due to this ignorance people remain passive and unbelieving.

b) Wrong teaching

In some circles people are taught that the gifts of the Holy Spirit were only intended for the first church in Acts and that God does not give them in these days. This is not what the Bible teaches us! If we take our calling and mission seriously we discover just how much we need the gifts of the Spirit! The Bible teaches us also that Jesus is still the same (Hebrews 13:8) and wants to fill us today with His Spirit and gifts.

iv) You must be willing to use your gifts

God's gifts are given for a specific purpose, i.e. to equip His Church. If it is your earnest desire to use the gift to the glory of God (and not so that you may be noticed by others), and you are willing to bear the cost, even of suffering and persecution, then God will give you His gifts.

v) You must pray

Many people want others to tell them what their gifts are. Whilst it is right to have gifting confirmed by others, it is God who gives them in the first place. It is to God, therefore, that we must come in prayer to receive confirmation of, and empowering in, His gifts. We will experience this when we pray, and we will have the assurance that it is indeed a gift of the Holy Spirit. Putting our gifts into practice therefore is, above all, a matter of prayer.

PART 7.3
'Eagerly Desire the Greater Gifts'

This is an exhortation given by Paul in 1 Corinthians 12:31 and 14:1. In Greek the word that has been translated *eagerly desire* is ***zeloo*** which means *burning with desire for something*, *to really long for it*, or *fall in love with it*. This does not mean making a strong effort in the flesh, but having a strong desire out of love for God. Besides having this strong desire there are some practical aids as well:

i) Study God's Word

The Bible is our source of inspiration as to how to practise our gifts. It not only teaches us what the different gifts are, but also what they are for and, last but not least, who the Giver is. We also find many examples as to how people have used their spiritual gifts.

ii) Do a lot of reading

There is a lot of literature available on the subject. Conferences are being held about this as well. Everybody has his own particular viewpoint and emphasis. Look at the different points of view and compare them with the Word of God. Our personal opinion should be formed and confirmed by what we find in the Word.

iii) Try to use the gift in your church

Even though it may not be possible to practise the gifts in the Sunday services, there should be scope for discovering and practising the gifts in small groups. Do not wait passively, but take initiatives and count on God's wisdom and guidance.

iv) Get to know other Christians who use their gifts

Mixing with Christians who use the gifts can be very stimulating and edifying. They can tell us how they have discovered their gifts and teach us how they have learned to use them. This might help us to become more confident too. Whilst we can learn from others, we must be careful that we do not just copy what other people are doing.

Personal Notes

PART 7.4
How to Discover the Gifts

The Scriptures show us that there is a distinction between the three groups of gifts:

i) Body gifts

The Body gifts are found in 1 Corinthians 12:8–10 and have been described extensively in Section 5. These are also called *extraordinary* or *supernatural* gifts. God gives us these gifts for the moment they are needed. Though always available, they become effective only when we open ourselves to receive them. They are given spontaneously, e.g. in meetings, but also when we meet someone with a particular need. They are needed in every ministry and are equally available to every church member.

ii) Personality gifts

These gifts are mentioned in Romans 12:6–8. They differ from the Body gifts by being more connected to our own personalities – our inherent characteristics – and so have a more permanent effect; e.g. the gift of leadership is not just for an instant, but will last as long as we have certain responsibilities. The following points may be helpful in discovering these gifts:

a) Be available

If you want to know whether you can swim you just have to try. If you look around in the church you will soon find a special need. It might be either a spiritual or practical need. Try to do something about it and reach out for God's power to meet that need. Be prepared to carry out any task in the church that you are asked to do. Sometimes we avoid certain assignments because we do not like to do them. That way we will never be able to discover our gifts. When you carry out a task just ask God to give you the gift needed for this task. God will confirm your gifts as you use them.

It can be quite a relief to discover that certain gifts are not ours. It will make us more open for those gifts that God actually does want to give us.

b) Be thankful

It is quite all right for us Christians to be happy when we perform our tasks within the church. Sometimes we think that doing God's will has to be hard, that it is meant to make us unhappy. However, when we serve in the gifts of the Spirit we begin to experience God's peace, and give thanks to God (Colossians 3:17).

c) What is the outworking?

Because the gifts are given for a purpose, we can expect there to be effects when we use them. If this does not happen we must ask whether we have received the particular gift. For example, someone with a gift for evangelism should see people being saved. When the gifts are functioning then the things we have been anticipating will truly happen.

d) Expect confirmation by the Body of Christ

Gifts need to be confirmed. Fruitfulness will confirm gifts, but they should also be recognised by other people in the church. If, apart from yourself, no-one else in the church can confirm your gifting, then most probably you are mistaken. This can cause a turmoil of feelings, however feelings are very deceptive and not to be relied on.

Having our gifts discovered and recognised by others has a very encouraging and stimulating effect, and leads to more opportunities to make use of the gifts.

iii) Gifts of service (ministry gifts)

Here we are dealing with the ministry gifts mentioned in Ephesians 4:11. The person who has one of these ministry callings carries the authority of that calling within himself and is recognised by more than one church. It is God who determines to whom a gift is given, and it is the church who will need to recognise and confirm this.

Personal Notes

Looking at Paul we see that he made use of teams. When he travelled around as an apostle, evangelist and teacher he took other people like Silas, Barnabas and Timothy with him. It appears most likely that Timothy's primary gifting was as pastor/teacher, but that he also had a secondary gifting as an evangelist, which he discovered while travelling with Paul (2 Timothy 4:5). He received his gifting when Paul laid hands on him, as recorded in 2 Timothy 1:6.

That is why it is so important that church elders themselves have received a ministry gift. This does not mean that every teacher or evangelist ought to be an elder, but that an elder should have at least one of the five ministry gifts. That is the way these ministry gifts will be multiplied in the church, just as they were in Paul's time (2 Timothy 2:2).

Before someone is appointed to leadership it should be evident in his manner and action that he qualifies for the position (1 Timothy 3:1–7).

PART 7.5
Characteristics of a Growing Church

W hen the gifts are operating within the church, the result will be growth and renewal through the work of the Holy Spirit. It is essential that the gifts and ministries have their proper place in the Body and that there is no imbalance.

A growing church has eight very important attributes. All eight are equally important, as there will not be a healthy growth of the church if one area is not fully developed.

These attributes are given below. Mark each of them in the box according to the way they function in your church using a scale of 1–10 (1 = non-existent; 10 = consistently exercised).

i)   Minister/Pastor

- gift of leadership
- gift of vision and faith

ii)   The ministry gifts of Ephesians 4:11 in church council or council of elders

- apostle
- prophet
- evangelist
- pastor
- teacher

Or is this the responsibility of the minister/pastor only?

iii) Is the church 'gifts-oriented'?
(as mentioned in Romans 12:3–8)

- leadership
- counselling
- acts of service
- teaching
- giving/mercy
- relief ministry
- children's ministry
- prayer ministry, etc.

iv) Enthusiasm in spiritual life

- living relationship with God
- discipleship
- dynamic life of faith
- being filled with the Holy Spirit
- openness for and functioning of the gifts (see 1 Corinthians 12:4–11)

v) Cell groups

- fellowship, edification
- care for one another
- open house (*oikos*)
- new visitors

vi) Functional structure and strategy

- make-up of the church
- location of the church
- identity of the church
- division of co-workers, dealing with talents
- vision and goals
- planning of campaigns

vii) Problem-oriented evangelism

- target groups
- visitation service
- evangelistic campaigns

viii) Love

- love is more than a feeling (commitment)
- love and care for one another
- love is the motivation for every activity

Looking at your own church, which do you think is the characteristic that needs most emphasis?

_____

_____

_____

Indicate why you think so.

_____

_____

_____

_____

Make the above mentioned characteristics a matter of prayer in your church, so that they can start taking shape!

Personal Notes

Bible Study: *Gifts of the Holy Spirit*

J esus came to make disciples. Disciples are children of God who want to follow Jesus by having their lives shaped to His likeness and by obeying His commission to make disciples of others (Romans 8:29). It has never been Jesus' intention to send His disciples out in their own strength, but He sends them out in His authority, in His power, in His ability and with His gifts.

In this study we want to take a closer look at the gifts of the Spirit which Jesus places at our disposal.

1. Just before His arrest Jesus said: *'It is for your good that I am going away'* (John 16:7a).

   What were the profound reasons that made Jesus say this? Write after each verse the reason mentioned:

   a) John 16:7b: _____

   _____

   b) John 16:12–15: _____

   _____

   c) Acts 1:8: _____

   _____

   d) Ephesians 4:8: _____

   _____

2. All spiritual gifts are gifts of grace that the Giver wants to give us because He loves us. What does that mean for us personally? (To find out read Romans 12:6; 1 Corinthians 12:4, 7 and 11.)

   _____

   _____

   _____

   _____

3. In the past the gifts of the Holy Spirit have sometimes caused envy and division within a church, because of the believers not being aware of the principle mentioned under Question 2. However, although the basic principle is *grace*; we still have our own responsibility. Do you know what that is? (1 Corinthians 12:31; 1 Corinthians 14:1):

    _____

    _____

    _____

    How do we receive the gifts? (1 Corinthians 12:31b–14:1a)

    _____

    _____

    _____

4. The purpose of receiving the gifts is to do the will of God.

    Jesus came to do His Father's will and it is His desire that we continue this work. In John 14:12 and 13 Jesus explains this to His disciples. Describe in your own words what is being said in these verses.

    _____

    _____

    _____

    _____

Personal Notes

Personal Notes

5. Though we might not realise it, God gave each one of us special talents when He made us. Try to discover your own talents and write them down below. Indicate alongside each talent whether you have consecrated this talent to God for His service and His glory. (Check either 'Yes' or 'No')

Talent	*Consecrated*
_____	○ Yes ○ No
_____	○ Yes ○ No
_____	○ Yes ○ No
_____	○ Yes ○ No

6. There is a clear difference between our natural talents and the gifts of the Spirit. Our natural talents we received at birth. After being born again and filled with the Spirit we receive spiritual gifts. Gifts of grace are given to Christians only, while anybody, be they Christian or non-Christian, may have talents.

    Try to find out what you think are gifts of the Spirit in your own life; something you do not have by nature, but something you feel inspired and enabled by God to do. Write them down:

    _____

    _____

    _____

    _____

    Are the gifts of grace functioning in your church, or are things done and organised only through natural talents? Define your answer:

    _____

    _____

    _____

    _____

7. The gifts of the Spirit are for the edification of the local church (Ephesians 4:11–13). We will take the ministry of Paul and Timothy as an example.

Read 1 Timothy 4:11–14 and 2 Timothy 4:5. What were Timothy's primary and secondary giftings?

_____

_____

What did Paul advise Timothy to do in order to develop his gift? (2 Timothy 1:6)

_____

_____

_____

In 2 Timothy 1:7 Paul mentions four characteristics of the gifts of the Holy Spirit. Name them:

a) _____

b) _____

c) _____

d) _____

Using your spiritual gifts is not without cost. In spite of that Paul calls Timothy to continue to obey.

What were the practical implications for Timothy? (verse 8).

_____

_____

_____

Every believer has been chosen to fulfil a specific task or calling (Ephesians 2:10). If we do not fulfil this task, we will:

_____

_____

Personal Notes

Paul knew his gifts, and that gave him confidence and authority in his calling. In 2 Timothy 1:11 Paul mentions his own gifts. Write them down:

a) _____

b) _____

c) _____

What was it that gave him the strength and the motivation not to be ashamed and to endure suffering? (verse 12)

_____

_____

_____

Paul had been faithful to his calling and was certain of his reward (2 Timothy 4:7, 8). Describe what is being said in these verses:

_____

_____

_____

8. In connection with receiving and developing the gifts of the Spirit the Bible gives the following instructions:

a) *Commitment*
    Read Romans 12:1 and define this commitment:

    _____

    _____

    _____

    What does this mean for you personally?

    _____

    _____

b) *Discovering God's will*
Romans 12:2 sets out a condition for discovering God's will. What condition is this?

_____

_____

One of the greatest blocks for the functioning of the gifts of the Spirit is our thinking. Sometimes God is wanting to use us through His gifts, but because of our deliberations and rational approach we are not open to His grace and power.

c) *Act in faith*
Another block is presumption and fanaticism. This also originates in our mind, in our imagination. Read Romans 12:3 and define Paul's warning:

_____

_____

_____

d) *Be filled with the Holy Spirit*
In Ephesians 5:17 Paul exhorts people to seek to do God's will. To do this we need to be filled with the Spirit of God (verse 18). This is also true for the gifts of the Spirit. Do you seek to be filled daily?

○   Yes

○   No

If your answer is 'No', why not?

_____

_____

e) ***Greatly desire the gifts***
Fill in the blanks (1 Corinthians 14:1):

'F_____

_____ *gifts.'*

This instruction we also find in 1 Corinthians 12:31.

In Greek the word translated *to desire eagerly* is **zeloo**, which implies: *having warmth of feeling for it, to really long for it, to fall in love with it.*

f) ***Fan the gift into flame***
It is possible to become passive, perhaps because of discouragement, opposition, unbelief or other reasons. What does Paul write to Timothy in 2 Timothy 1:6?

_____

The gift will always remain a gift of the Spirit. Therefore we continually need to give the Spirit access to our lives and allow the fire of the Holy Spirit to fan our gifts into flame.

9. Which of the instructions under Question 8 is/are new to you?

_____

_____

_____

Which instruction(s) do you need to pay more attention to?

_____

_____

_____

Answers

1. a) Because then the Counsellor, the Holy Spirit, will come.
    b) The Holy Spirit will guide into all truth, and bring glory to Jesus.
    c) The Holy Spirit will give power to witness.
    d) So that people would receive (ministry) – gifts.

2. We cannot claim the gifts, they are given to us by grace, that no-one may boast. God gives them to His Church with a purpose in mind, that they might be for the praise of His glory.

3. To eagerly desire the gifts, to go after them.

    Through love. Love strengthens faith (Galatians 5:6) creates an openness in our lives for the gifts, and makes us respect and appreciate one another.

4. The charge is to continue the commission Jesus had. He went to the Father and He was glorified, which made it possible for the Holy Spirit to come with all the gifts to prepare us for this commission.

5. Personal

6. Personal

    Personal

7. Timothy had the giftings of pastor/teacher and evangelist.

    To fan his gift into flame; to let it grow; to take his gift seriously

    a) not timid
    b) loving
    c) powerful
    d) self-disciplined (sound)

    Suffering may be the consequence.

    Miss God's purpose for our lives.

a) Herald
b) Apostle
c) Teacher

Paul had a keen sense of the calling he received from his Master (Galatians 1:12, 15, 16) and was determined to remain faithful to it until the day of his death; he knew Christ would supply all the strength needed.

Paul loved Jesus till the end and showed this in his faithfulness and obedience to his calling. He knew therefore that the crown of righteousness was awaiting him.

8. a) To offer our lives completely to Christ; to be at His service because we love Him; to be an acceptable, God-pleasing sacrifice.

Personal

b) By turning our backs on worldly principles, bending our thoughts towards God and being renewed in our minds (1 Corinthians 2:10–16).
c) Without sober judgement (wisdom) we do not take into account God's will. We then run the risk of not acting in faith.
d) Personal
e) See 1 Corinthians 14:1
f) *'Fan into flame the gift of God.'*

9. Personal

SECTION 8
How to Develop a Ministry Gift

Personal Notes

Introduction

To receive a gift (any of the gifts) is only the beginning. It is absolutely essential that our gifting continues to develop, but what do we mean by *develop*? Does it mean that we become more capable, more experienced, more knowledgeable? Although this will happen, it is not completely what we mean. When we speak of development, of growth, we are speaking about the principle of the grain of wheat.

> *'I tell you the truth, unless a grain of wheat falls to the ground and dies, it remains only a single seed. **But if it dies, it produces many seeds**.'* (John 12:24)

This has everything to do with brokenness. It is about knowing God's grace, our close relationship with the Father, the renewal of our mind, the moulding of our character and the way we handle our time and money. To develop a gift is not cheap, it requires one's full devotion. In this section we will take a closer look at the principles for growth and development.

Key Verses

Proverbs 13:12, 19   Romans 12:9–21

Philippians 3:14   1 Corinthians 15:10

Ephesians 4:20–32   1 Corinthians 2:10–16

PART 8.1
The Outworking of Grace

A (ministry) gift is the outworking of God's grace in and through our lives. The grace of God is the basis on which our lives and our service for Him are built (Ephesians 1:3–6). As Christians we all have our own specific ministry or calling (Ephesians 2:10). There are distinctions, but they are all equally important.

God's desire is for us to be His co-workers. The following points show us how we can be channels for God's grace to flow out to others.

- God has a purpose for your life and for your church.

- He calls us to fulfil His purpose. That is what His gifts are for.

- Our responsibility is to be committed.

- Our commitment is the key that starts the flow of God's grace.

- God's grace makes the use of the gifts effective.

- By being effective our authority is enhanced and so we receive power.

- This encourages us to step out in works of faith.

In other words, firstly we must find out what God's will is. Secondly we must accept God's grace to do His will. Finally, we must put it into practise and step out in faith, so that God's purpose is actually being accomplished.

We recognise God's grace because of its effect in our daily lives. To Paul God's grace was the important motivating force in everything he did. Like others, he had discovered God's grace in his life and knew the meaning of it

> *'But by the grace of God I am what I am, and his grace to me was not without effect. No, I worked harder than all of them – yet not I, but the grace of God that was with me.'* (1 Corinthians 15:10)

PART 8.2
How to Be Effective

'I press on towards the goal to win the prize for which God has called me heavenwards in Christ Jesus.'
(Philippians 3:14)

A computer cannot predict the future; it can work out plans for the future but this depends completely on the information that has been fed into it. In the same way it is possible for our past to so shape our future that it prevents us from being open to the new things that God wants to do. We must be careful not to act only according to what we have experienced and the information we have been given. We should not be dependent on our knowledge and experience alone, lest we allow the past to determine our future.

We can miss reaching the goal in our ministry by trying to do things our own way and in our own strength. Before we can be effective, God needs to break our self-confidence and independence. He wants servants who are eager to do His will and know they are dependent on the Holy Spirit.

The following points are important to a fruitful ministry:

- An awareness that it is God's work and that we are totally dependent on the work of the Holy Spirit (2 Corinthians 3:4–6).

- It is of prime importance that our minds are being made new (Ephesians 4:20–24). We cannot trust old habits, traditions or experience.

- The Holy Spirit knows what is in God's heart and He wants to reveal it to us (1 Corinthians 2:10–16). It is very important that our spirit is open to what God's Spirit is telling us.

- The love of Christ should be the motivating force of our lives (2 Corinthians 5:14). The most effective Christians are those whose service for God flows from the fact that they know Him and love Him. They do not work for money, status, reputation, power, honour, or any other self-centred aim. Pure motivations will help us to stand a lot of pressure, and make us more willing to sacrifice our lives to God.

- God is looking for people who will serve Him without needing to prove themselves. He is looking for people who can rest in their relationship of faith with Him.

A Christian can bring God into a situation through the gifts of the Holy Spirit, and thereby live a much more fruitful life. This sets us free from the need to have everything worked out and under control.

PART 8.3
Serving with Gladness

P leasing ourselves and our selfish desires does not give us joy; joy is the fruit of serving God and others. True servants of God know this. To be busy with satisfying our own desires is the opposite of having a servant heart.

God calls us to serve Him with gladness – serving Him reluctantly does not please Him. Serving God joyfully will help us to stay in good health and to keep our motives pure, so that the peace of God will guard our hearts (Philippians 4:4–9; Colossians 3:15–17). This will help us to develop our ministry gifting.

> '*Delight yourself in the Lord and He will give you the desires of your heart. Commit your way to the Lord; trust in Him and He will do this.*' (Psalm 37:4, 5)

PART 8.4
Our Character

There may be some natural character traits or motivations in our lives that cause the development of our ministry gift to be stunted.

Questions

The following questions refer to:

- your job

- your relationships

- your personal desires

- your spiritual ministry

Answer the following questions:

- When God/the church asks you to do something, will you do it?

  _____

  _____

- Do you usually complete the things that you have begun?

  _____

  _____

- Does your life show failure after failure? If so, why is it like that?

  _____

  _____

  _____

- Have failures, or difficult circumstances, made you feel insecure?

  _____

  _____

- Do you change jobs frequently because you do not get any satisfaction out of your work? If so, do you know why?

  _____

  _____

- Which of the following factors *have been a hindrance* in trying to achieve certain aims in your life?

  - no motivation

  - no clear goals

  - no realistic planning

  - no prospects

  - no support

  - no faith

  - no training/discipleship

  - no encouragement

  Mention these factors below:

  _____

  _____

  _____

  _____

- What factors *have helped* you to achieve a certain goal?

  _____

  _____

  _____

  _____

'Two people were looking out of a prison; one saw only mud, the other saw the sun.'

When God gives us an open door we must go on and, in the power of the Holy Spirit, do the things God shows us. How many Christians are waiting on the steps outside an open door? How many Christians have not yet found this open door? How many Christians are retreating through the back door?

'A longing fulfilled is sweet to the soul.'
(Proverbs 13:19)

'Hope deferred makes the heart sick, but a longing fulfilled is a tree of life.' (Proverbs 13:12)

PART 8.5
Intimacy with God

Those who sought an intimate relationship with God have been the most fruitful of all. There are many examples of servants whose first priority was to seek God for who He is, for His blessings, and for the baptism in the Holy Spirit.

In Psalm 25:14 David says:

> 'The Lord confides in those who fear Him; He makes His covenant known to them.'

And in Psalm 27:4 he says:

> 'One thing I ask of the Lord, this is what I seek: that I may dwell in the house of the Lord all the days of my life, to gaze upon the beauty of the Lord and to seek him in his temple.'

This means spending time with the Father. All preachers or missionaries who made this a priority experienced growth in their ministries and were greatly blessed. The evangelist D.L. Moody gave the following testimony of such a time with God:

> 'I persisted in calling out to God to fill me with His Holy Spirit. Then, one day in New York – oh glorious day – I cannot describe it and hardly ever talk about it; it is almost too holy an experience to mention. The apostle Paul had an experience he did not talk about until 14 years later. I can only say that God revealed Himself to me. I experienced His love in such a way that I had to ask Him to stay His hand. I went back to preaching. My preaching was no different; I did not preach new things: and yet hundreds of people turned to the Lord.'

Do we desire to grow in our ministry? Then we will have to spend time with the Father. This was David's secret. What is more, it was the secret of the ministry of the Lord Jesus. See Luke 5:16 & 17b; 6:12; 9:29 & 11:1.

Assignment

I n order to become effective in one's ministry the following questions are very important.

Just remember: the purpose of these questions is not to make you feel guilty, but to help you test your motivations and priorities.

1. Who do you serve? Discover whom or what you really are serving, by answering the following questions as honestly as possible.

    •   What has first place in your life? What are your priorities?

        _____

        _____

        _____

    •   Which things take most of your time?

        _____

        _____

        _____

    •   What would be the last thing you would give up?

        _____

        _____

        _____

    •   What are the things you have set your heart on?

        _____

        _____

        _____

- What do you spend most of your money on?

  _____

  _____

  _____

- Which things occupy your mind most?

  _____

  _____

  _____

- Where is your treasure? (There your heart will be also, according to Matthew 6:19–24.)

  _____

  _____

  _____

- Are you serving two or more masters?

  _____

  _____

  _____

2. You may want to use the following questions for a regular personal check-up:

    - Am I willing to be God's servant and let this shape the rest of my life?

      _____

      _____

      _____

    - Am I willing to daily pay the price to serve God and others?

      _____

      _____

- Am I willing to live the life God requires of me as His disciple and to be an example to others?

  _____

  _____

  _____

- Am I willing to give up everything for God's sake and to do all He asks of me, whatever the cost?

  _____

  _____

  _____

- Am I prepared to encourage others to develop fully in their service for God, even if it means that they will develop more than I do in certain areas?

  _____

  _____

  _____

- Am I prepared to learn and to listen to others?

  _____

  _____

  _____

- Like Jesus, are you submissive to the will of God?

  _____

  _____

  _____

- As servants we need to be conformed to the likeness of Jesus. Study the life of Jesus as portrayed in the Gospels and follow His example. What are the areas that need to be worked on?

  _____

  _____

  _____

- Are you prepared to do the things that may not seem so important? What is your motivation for the ministry? Is it to help others and serve them, or is it to be well-known, or to be served yourself? Is your motivation the same as the one mentioned in Matthew 22:37–39 and Philippians 2:1–8?

  _____

  _____

  _____

- Are you able to trust God with your life, or do you want to help Him? Are you striving?

  _____

  _____

  _____

- Can God trust you?

  _____

  _____

- Are you willing to let Jesus take first place in all areas of your life? Can you say that you have been crucified with Christ and that you no longer live, but that Christ lives in you? (Galatians 2:20) If not, why not?

  _____

  _____

  _____

- Who gets the credit for all that you do? Of which kingdom are you a servant?

  _____

  _____

  _____

- After you have answered these questions it would be good to ask the Holy Spirit the question: 'Is there anything in my life that needs to change, so that I may serve God and others even better?' Write down what He shows you, and your response.

  _____

  _____

  _____

  _____

  _____

SECTION 9
Private and Corporate Prayer

Personal Notes

Introduction

In this section we will look at private and corporate prayer. Prayer is essential for our spiritual lives as well as for all church-related activities. Due to lack of prayer much work is without fruit and has no power. The same applies to leaders. Often the workload is heavy and poses a real threat to our prayer life. Acts 6:4 shows us that the first church leaders knew their priorities.

Prayer simply means talking with God. In prayer God speaks to us and we speak to Him; He listens to us and we listen to Him. Prayer is more than just asking. Prayer also means: listening to God, praising, worshipping Him, giving Him thanks, waiting for Him, interceding, being engaged in spiritual warfare.

We should not pray because we are forced into it, or to do God a favour; it is a privilege to pray. In prayer we can come into the presence of God our Father. This holy and almighty God delights in meeting with us.

By praying we cannot change God's character or mind. God is unchanging, He remains forever the same. Prayer can, however, change us! Prayer changes the one who prays; the result is a channel through which God's blessing can flow.

Through prayer the Kingdom of God is revealed. That is why satan is afraid of people who pray.

Key Verses

Matthew 6:5–18	Hebrews 10:19–22
Luke 11:1–13	Philippians 4:6, 7
Romans 8:26–27	Mark 11:22–25
Ephesians 6:18	1 John 5:14–15

PART 9.1
The Lord's Prayer

J esus prayed a lot to His Father. His prayer life was so inspiring that His disciples asked Him:

> *'Lord, teach us to pray.'* (Luke 11:1)

That is when Jesus taught them what we call *The Lord's prayer* (Luke 11:2–4; Matthew 6:9–13). This prayer is often viewed as a standard prayer or collect, however this is not what it is meant for. Jesus gave this prayer as an example, and in it He mentions all the elements a prayer should have.

We find *The Lord's Prayer* in Matthew 6:9–13 and it has the following elements:

i) Worship

Worship is the first element (verses 9–10). Jesus teaches us to focus our eyes on God.

In our worship we can focus on:

- the love of God the Father

- the holiness of God

- the omnipotence, the enormous power of God

- God's faithfulness to His promises

When we worship God we prepare the way for God's salvation (Psalm 50:23). Also in Psalm 37:4 God gives a rich promise:

> *'Delight yourself in the LORD*
> *and **he will give you the desires of your heart**.'*

ii) **Supplication**

Through worship we have confidence to pray for our daily needs (verses 11–13a). When we focus on God, He will:

- reveal to us our sins

- reveal whether our relationship with Himself and/or others is not right

- give us insight into how we can pray for our daily needs

- give us promises from His Word to build up our faith

Sincerely confessing our sins clears the way for us to pray with confidence and in faith.

iii) **Thanksgiving**

In verse 13b the prayer ends with praise and thanksgiving. It is a proclamation of faith in the victory of God. By doing so we place the responsibility for answered prayer in God's hands. With this proclamation we can confess:

- that Jesus is Lord over all

- that He has all power

- that His name will be glorified

Faith is the ingredient that gives us the peace and confidence that God will bring it to pass.

It is very important that our prayers contain these three elements. However, each prayer is different, and these elements may be present in a different form.

PART 9.2
Jesus Made Prayer a Priority

Jesus urged us to pray (Matthew 9:38), and He prayed continually. Even Jesus, in His ministry, was totally dependent on His Father's will and the power of the Holy Spirit (see Luke 6:12 & 11:1).

Prayer is the real work.

> '*But Jesus often withdrew to lonely places and prayed.*'
> (Luke 5:16)

In the following verse we read what happened as a result of His prayer life:

> '*And the power of the Lord was present for Him to heal the sick.*'
> (Luke 5:17)

Prayer changes lives. Jesus experienced this in Luke 9:29:

> '*As He was praying, the appearance of his face changed, and his clothes became as bright as a flash of lightning.*'

Through prayer we are in touch with heaven, which makes us a channel for God's glory on earth (Luke 3:21; John 15:1–8).

> *Jesus persisted in prayer until He knew that His prayer was answered.*

While doing so His focus was always on discovering the will of the Father (Luke 22:39–45).

PART 9.3
Victorious Prayer

i) What do we mean by victorious prayer?

- Victorious prayer is not just having good and pure desires; neither does it equal expressed desires. There is more to it.

- Victorious prayer is the prayer that God has made powerful and effective (James 5:16).

- Victorious prayer is the prayer that receives the blessing which was prayed for. Promises become reality.

ii) What are the characteristics of victorious prayer?

a) It is specific

We cannot expect victory when we pray in a haphazard kind of way. We should be clear in our minds about what we want to pray for and not pray for everything at the same time. There are many examples of victorious prayer in the Bible, and in each case people had a specific goal in mind.

b) It is according to God's will

Victorious prayer is prayer that expresses God's will. Prayers which are not in accordance with God's will do not bring victory. We can discover God's will for our prayers through:

- *Specific and clear promises in God's Word*. These may be promises for something specific as well as general promises which we may claim in particular cases (1 Timothy 2:3, 4; 1 John 5:15).

- *Special events in everyday life*. In that way God may warn us or point out something which is going to happen. He makes this clear to those who have spiritual discernment (Acts 16:1–10).

- *The Holy Spirit*. When we do not know how to pray the Holy Spirit will teach us (Romans 8:26, 27). That is why it is so important to be filled with the Holy Spirit. The Spirit will lead us into praying for the things God wants to answer.

c) It flows from a humble heart

Being submissive does not mean being indifferent, or having a general kind of confidence that God is going to do what is best anyway. What it does mean, is that we receive and accept the will of God. As long as we are not clear about God's will we should not give up praying. We only can be submissive to the revealed will of God. Submission to an assumed will of God is not submission at all. David's prayer in 2 Samuel 12:16–23 is an example of this. Therefore it is important that we do not assume facts beforehand. If we do, how can we be sure that God will be merciful to us?

d) It flows from pure motives

Do we pray for selfish reasons, or because we feel sorry for people? Instead of praying because God's Name is being dishonoured, we could be praying for the lost just because we feel sorry for them. The highest motive we must have is God's honour and His Kingdom, and this brings victory (James 4:1–4).

e) It is under the guidance of the Holy Spirit

Without the Holy Spirit's intervention we will not be able to pray effectively. We need the Holy Spirit, for example:

- *To pray in accordance with God's will*. It is the Spirit who reveals God's will to us. Only the Spirit knows the thoughts of God and wants to reveal them to us (1 Corinthians 2:10–16). To sense God's will does not mean having a fictitious desire; rather, it is an inward assurance because God's Spirit testifies with our spirit that this is God's will. This creates assurance and faith.

Personal Notes

- *To pray persistently*. To discover God's will is the first step, but then we must pray with perseverance (Hebrews 10:35, 36). This is where our problem lies, not because we do not know this but because we fail to do it; or we stop praying too early, without having received the blessing.

f) It is by faith

We need faith to have victory in prayer (Mark 11:22–24; 1 John 5:4). Faith is a gift of the Holy Spirit. It is not an imagined assurance, but it rests on the revealed will of God. Faith is more than just hoping, it is the inner assurance of things hoped for. Prayer makes the invisible visible (Hebrews 11:1–3). We do not only believe *something* will happen, we believe that the specific things we asked for in faith will happen (Luke 11:1–13).

g) It is persistent

It is quite hard not to be distracted, to keep our minds on the things we pray for. Through the Spirit of prayer our hearts must become heavy with the burden and the vision God gives us, so that we are determined to continue in prayer until we have received victory (Zechariah 12:10; Luke 18:1–8; 22:39–46; Acts 4:23–31). This does not mean that we always receive the victory after praying just once, sometimes we need to pray for a longer period of time.

h) It is empowered with the authority of Jesus

Victorious prayer must be offered in the name of Jesus Christ. Jesus made available to us the authority of His name. This does not mean that we just *automatically* close a prayer with: 'In Jesus' name. Amen.' It implies that we will remain in Him, obey Him and follow Him (John 15:1–17).

PART 9.4
Hindrances to Victorious Prayer

W e know that prayer is very important, and yet in practice we experience many hindrances. Some of these hindrances have to do with ourselves:

- not paying attention to the Word (Proverbs 28:9)

- unconfessed sins (Isaiah 59:1–2)

- worry, fear (Matthew 6:25–34)

- no unity (Matthew 18:19–20)

- unforgiveness (Mark 11:25)

- living unholy lives (1 Timothy 2:8)

- doubt/unbelief (James 4:3)

- marriage problems (1 Peter 3:7)

- lack of insight regarding the times in which we live (1 Peter 4:7)

- not praying according to God's will (1 John 5:14, 15)

Personal guilt as well as collective guilt can be a hindrance. Nehemiah not only confessed his own sins, but also those of the entire nation (Nehemiah 1:6b–7).

PART 9.5
Steps in Personal and Corporate Prayer

a) Relax, and focus your eyes on God (Psalm 46:11). The following things will stimulate you in doing this: praise and worship; reading the Word of God and meditating upon it; an awareness of God's greatness, power and love. In the beginning this will call for self-discipline, but eventually it will become a joy to do it. Choose a time of day or night in which you probably will not be disturbed. Be sure to not only have time enough to talk to God, but also to listen to Him.

b) Confess every sin that the Holy Spirit reveals to you and receive God's forgiveness (1 John 1:9). We also must forgive those who have hurt us. After that we may accept God's cleansing and then we will know that our hearts are clean before Him (Matthew 5:8; Psalm 24:3–6).

c) Pray for the baptism in the Holy Spirit (Ephesians 5:18). Ask in faith for the Holy Spirit to empower you, to guide you and to pray through you. Speaking in tongues may be helpful.

d) Make sure you are protected. Satan wants to hinder our prayer life, or attack us personally. According to James 4:6–7 the following is important for protection:

- be humble

- be confident of God's grace

- submit yourself to God

- resist the devil

To resist the devil we should ask for the covering of the blood of Jesus and use the name of Jesus. God also made available to us His whole armour (Ephesians 6:8–10) (see Section 4).

e)   If you expect God to speak to you, you must wait for Him. (Psalm 62:6; Micah 7:7). There are three voices that may influence your mind when you are praying: your own, satan's and God's. Therefore it is necessary that we:

- submit our minds and wills to God

- are cleansed by the blood of Christ

- are filled with the Holy Spirit

f)   Be obedient. If God puts something on your heart to pray for, or to say to Him or to others, speak it out.

g)   Persist in prayer until you know that your prayer has been answered and you receive God's peace in your heart (Philippians 4:7). Do not go by your feelings. There may be days that you find it very hard to pray and that you do not seem to be getting through. Do not give up, continue to pray and God will bless you, and you will again experience His presence.

h)   Be yourself when you pray. It is unnecessary to use formal, pious language, or to speak in a special kind of voice. God is your Father and He loves you as you are.

i)   Do not be anxious, but cast all your care on Christ (1 Peter 5:7). It is a sin to worry, for it shows a lack of trust in your Heavenly Father (Matthew 6:25–34). Have faith in God when you pray.

j)   Be specific in your prayers, for God wants to give specific answers. A prayer list may be of help. Praying out loud may help to keep your mind from wandering.

k)   Alternate your prayer with praise and worship.

l)   Combine prayer with fasting. Prayer that is accompanied by fasting is more powerful. It does not mean that you want to force God into something, but it is a way of self-denial and discipline so that there may be more of God and less of yourself.

PART 9.6
Fasting and Prayer

The Hebrew word for fasting is **tsuwm**, which means *to cover one's mouth*. In Greek the word **nesteuo** is used, which means *abstaining from food voluntarily*.

Our motivation plays an important role in fasting. In Zechariah 7:5 the Lord is asking:

> 'When you fasted ... was it really for me that you fasted?'

In Matthew 6:18 Jesus is saying:

> '...so that it will not be obvious to men that you are fasting, **but only to your Father, who is unseen.**'

> First of all fasting is **a service to God, an act of worship and devotion**.

In practice there are also wrong motivations such as:

- wanting to do something to influence God

- wanting to be more spiritual than others

The most important objectives for fasting are:

- *Fellowship with God*
  Like prayer, fasting is something between God and us (Matthew 6:16–18).

- *Sanctification*
  Fasting plays an important role in humiliation and confession of sin (Nehemiah 1:4–11; Daniel 9:3–5).

- *To make our voice be heard by God*
  In Isaiah 58:4 the Lord says:

  > 'You cannot fast as you do today to make your voice to be heard on high.'

God wants us to ask of Him with all of our heart. He wants to make sure we are serious about it; that it is important to us as well, and not just a matter of words. Sincere fasting reveals the deep desires of our heart.

- **To turn away God's judgement**
  In Joel 2:12 the Lord calls on the people to repent. Fasting plays an important role in this.

    *'Return to me with all your heart, **with fasting** and weeping and mourning.'*

For example: 2 Samuel 12:15–17.

- **For deliverance**
  In Matthew 17:19 the disciples ask Jesus:

    'Why couldn't we drive it out?'

To which Jesus replies in verse 21:

    'But this kind does not go out except by prayer and fasting.'

Conclusion

Prayer and the Word of God are indissolubly linked together. If we pray in accordance with God's will we have the promise that we will see the answer (1 John 5:14–15; Romans 8:26–27). It is therefore of vital importance that we spend time with God and His Word. *Prayer links us to the unlimited possibilities of the Almighty God* (Psalms 2:8; 81:11; Jeremiah 33:3).

Summary and Application

1.   Prayer is communication between God and man.

2.   God always answers those prayers that are according to His will.

3.   To pray is a privilege and enhances our spiritual growth.

4.   As a child of God you pray to your loving heavenly Father who delights in giving to His children.

5.   Pray under the guidance of the Holy Spirit, for in doing so your prayer will be inspired by God Himself.

6.   Jesus made prayer a priority and so should we.

Prayer is the engine room of our work. Others have said: 'Prayer is the work.' The following Bible Study, **'Prayer'**, shows us what the practical outworking of prayer can be.

Bible Study: *Prayer*

I n the Bible we come across many examples of prayer. These examples teach us important lessons, and will motivate us to give high priority to prayer in our lives.

1. Jesus was a Man of prayer. He needed prayer to accomplish His commission. In the following verses we will find some examples. Write behind each verse the *objective* of Jesus' prayer:

    a) John 5:30 _____

    b) Luke 22:39–45 _____

    c) Luke 22:31–32 _____

    What was the *result* of Jesus' prayer in:

    d) Luke 5:16, 17b _____

    e) Luke 6:12–13 _____

    f) Luke 9:29 _____

    g) Mark 1:35–39 _____

2. What question did the disciples ask in Luke 11:1?

    _____

    _____

3. An example in the Old Testament of a man with a powerful prayer life is Nehemiah (Nehemiah 1:4–11). Read his prayer and insert the appropriate characteristics in the spaces below.

    a) Nehemiah 1:4–6a _____

    b) Nehemiah 1:6b–7 _____

    c) Nehemiah 1:8–10 _____

    d) Nehemiah 1:11 _____

4. Nehemiah's prayer of faith had quite an influence on people and circumstances. The next verses bring out these influences. Mention them after each person or event.

a) Nehemiah 2:6: The king _____

   _____

   _____

b) Nehemiah 2:10: The enemies _____

   _____

   _____

c) Nehemiah 2:20: Nehemiah himself _____

   _____

   _____

d) Nehemiah 3, and 4:6: The people _____

   _____

   _____

e) Nehemiah 6:15: The wall _____

   _____

   _____

f) Nehemiah 6:16: The enemies _____

   _____

   _____

5. Another example is Daniel's prayer (see Daniel 9:4–19). Study this prayer and compare its characteristics with those found in the prayer in Nehemiah 1 (see Question 3).

   _____

   _____

   _____

   _____

6. What was it that Daniel started to pray for (Daniel 9:1–2; Jeremiah 29:10)?

_____

_____

_____

In which year did Daniel pray?

_____

_____

What happened in the second year of King Darius (Haggai 1:1; Zechariah 1:1)?

_____

_____

_____

What was the result of the ministry of these two prophets (Ezra 4:24–5:2; 6:14–15)?

_____

_____

_____

_____

The moment Daniel began to discover the promises in God's Word and started to pray about them, the fulfilment of those promises began!

7. To pray is to fight for the Kingdom of God. It is a spiritual battle and therefore there is spiritual opposition. Read Daniel 10:12–13.

Who wanted to prevent the answer to this prayer?

_____

_____

_____

8.   The Kingdom of God is shown through Jesus' ministry on earth. In the following passages we see victory gained through prayer or through a word of authority.

Jot down after each verse what Jesus gained victory over.

a)   Matthew 8:14–17 _____

_____

_____

b)   Matthew 8:26 _____

_____

_____

c)   Matthew 9:23–25 _____

_____

_____

d)   Matthew 14:19 _____

_____

_____

9.   The New Testament teaches us to pray in the Name of Jesus. In the Bible a name describes the whole person, his characteristics, personality and power.

What promise is given in John 14:12?

_____

_____

_____

Who is going to work these things out (verse 13b)?

_____

_____

What is our personal responsibility in this, according to:

- John 14:13a _____

  _____

  _____

- John 6:29 _____

  _____

  _____

We can do this during our private prayer time, but also when we pray (with the laying on of hands) for others. This is the way in which the Holy Spirit continues the work of Jesus.

10. With the help of James 5:16 fill in the blanks:

    'Therefore confess _____

    _____ *and* _____

    _____ *, so that*

    _____ *.*

    The prayer of _____

    _____ *.'*

11. What about you, do you have a desire for a deeper and more powerful prayer ministry?

    ◯ Yes

    ◯ No

Answers

1. a) He sought to do the will of the Father.
    b) To be obedient to the will of the Father.
    c) For perseverance in the faith of His disciples.
    d) Jesus received power in His ministry.
    e) Jesus chose His 12 disciples.
    f) God's glory was manifested in His life.
    g) The Gospel was preached, and evil spirits were cast out.

2. *'Lord, teach us to pray.'*

3. a) His focus is on God, he worships Him.
    b) He humbles himself, confesses his sins.
    c) In faith he reminds God of His promises.
    d) He is willing to be personally involved.

4. a) The king is willing to co-operate.
    b) Opposition from the enemy (prayer results in spiritual resistance).
    c) Nehemiah's prayer gave him faith, courage and determination.
    d) The people are as one and work with all their heart.
    e) The wall is finished within 52 days, in spite of the opposition.
    f) All the surrounding nations become afraid; they realise it is done with the help of God.

5. This prayer has the same characteristics as in Question 3.

6. Daniel prayed for the promised return and rebuilding of the temple.

    He prayed his prayer in the first year of Darius.

    In the second year of King Darius God called the prophets Haggai and Zechariah to speak to the people.

    The people started building again and the restoration was completed (at the right time).

7.   The prince of the Persian kingdom; a spiritual hostile power.

8.   a)   Over diseases and evil spirits.
     b)   Over death.
     c)   Over nature, wind and sea.
     d)   Over lack of food.

9.   That through faith in Jesus we will continue to do His works.

     Jesus says: 'I will do it.'

     •   To pray in the name of Jesus.
     •   To believe in Jesus.

10. See James 5:16.

11. Personal

SECTION 10
Prayer in Ministry

Introduction

In Section 9 we talked about our personal prayer life and about praying with others. In this section we will speak about praying with others during a time of ministry. By a *time of ministry* we mean the imparting of God's blessing and power into the lives of the people we are praying for. God wants to use us to bless, heal, fill and equip others. This happens by being a channel for the Holy Spirit and takes place through prayer.

Our ministry becomes effective through effective prayer. If we get to grips with the simplicity and power of the gift of prayer, then we will discover that this ministry is open to every one of us. We will start doing this when we become confident that God actually does answer our prayers. What God is looking for is openness to His working, so that He can work through us and use us in whatever situation He chooses to put us. We are representatives of the Kingdom of God. God wants us to be available to Him and through this ministry of prayer, to release His blessings into the lives and circumstances of the people around us every day.

Key Verses

James 5:13–18   John 14:12–14

Mark 7:31–35   Mark 6:41–44

Mark 10:13–16   Acts 5:12–16

Acts 6:3–4

PART 10.1
The Power of Prayer

John Wesley once said:

> 'It seems that God is limited by our prayer life – that He can do nothing for humanity unless someone asks Him.'

God has chosen to limit Himself to working through human beings like you and me. Through our prayers we can become a channel for God's blessing to others.

In John 14:12 Jesus makes it clear that His disciples will carry on His work. Jesus also tells us how this is possible, by giving the example of the *'true vine'* (John 15:1–8). By being a branch we become a channel for God's blessing. The focus, however, is on prayer:

> *'And I will do whatever you ask in my name ...'*
> (John 14:13)

> *'... ask whatever you wish, and it will be given you.'*
> (John 15:7)

Through the use of our prayer ministry, God's blessing is released into other people's lives.

PART 10.2
The Privilege of Prayer

The New Testament has the following words for *prayer*:

- *Deomai* – The meaning of this word is *to request, ask, plead,* or *pray*. This has to do with asking for help in relation to a certain need or want.

  > *'Teacher, I beg you to look at my son.'*
  > (Luke 9:38.)

- *Erotao* – This word means *to ask* (for), *to ask a question* (regarding).

  > *'I pray for them ... for those you have given me...'*
  > (John 17:9)

- *Aiteo* – This word also means *to ask* (in order to receive), *to pray*.

  > *'If you believe, you will receive whatever you ask for in prayer.'*
  > (Matthew 21:22)

The effectiveness of our ministry with other people may lie in the fact that we take the courage to ask them if we can pray with them. God gives us the privilege to pray to Him. We may come to Him with and for other people and ask Him to act in that particular situation or need.

The secret of this simple prayer of power is our relationship with the Father. It is God Himself who makes our words powerful (James 5:16). On the basis of this relationship of love with our all-powerful heavenly Father we are able to put our requests to Him.

PART 10.3
The Responsibility of Prayer

Another word for *prayer* in the New Testament is:

- *proseuchomai* – This means *to pour out* or *to persist in prayer*. Prayer is not an option for the disciple, but a responsibility and a commission. This is what God looks for – prayers that come from the depths of our being, and gain the victory through perseverance.

  'He told His disciples a parable to show them that they should always pray and not give up.'

  (Luke 18:1)

  'And pray in the Spirit on all occasions with all kinds of prayers and requests.' (Ephesians 6:18)

PART 10.4
The Effectiveness of Prayer

God has chosen prayer through believing Christians as an instrument for the revelation of who He is.

The Father is waiting for us to do His will. He wants to accomplish His purposes through our lives. His call through Ezekiel (Ezekiel 22:30) was for people who would stand in the gap for others, to save the people from destruction. Our world today is full of destruction and is heading for destruction. God wants to use us to deliver men and women from this and to bring them into the Kingdom of His Son (Colossians 1:13).

Therefore prayer has to do with conflict. Prayer, in fact, is the deciding factor in a spiritual conflict. The scene of the conflict is the earth. The purpose of the conflict is to show that Jesus has control over the earth and its inhabitants.

Every time we pray for another person we are helping to save them from the control of satan and deliver them from spiritual bondage. They are then in a place where they can receive God's glory, His Spirit, gifts and fullness. Each time it is another bit of territory claimed for Christ. This way the Kingdom of God is revealed in our own lives, in the Church and in this world.

PART 10.5
The Exercise of Prayer

T he whole secret of praying with other people is to be open to the leading and prompting of the Holy Spirit. Experience is a great teacher and we will soon become far more acute to the needs of each situation through the leading of the Holy Spirit.

It is essential that there is humility of heart and dependency on the Holy Spirit.

There are four levels of prayer when ministering to others:

a)   *Prayer with*
     This is where we identify with the other person in their request to the Father and agree with them in faith that their prayer will be answered (Matthew 18:19).

b)   *Prayer for*
     This is where we have identified the needs of the other person and bring them into the presence of God through prayer (James 5:16).

c)   *Prayer into*
     In this prayer God must be our focus. When He gives us a word for a specific situation we can speak it into that situation with authority. Through the Holy Spirit this word will become living and effective in that situation or person (Acts 3:6).

d)   *Prayer against*
     Sometimes we are led by the Spirit of God into an area of spiritual warfare and resistance. Here, there must be strong humility of spirit and a deep dependency on the leading of the Holy Spirit. The prayer is a movement of resistance against the spiritual realities of evil. It is important to call on the Lord in this situation and ask Him to rebuke satan because you are the represent-ative of Jesus in this situation.

Personal Notes

The place to start prayer for others is by listening to the other person within your spirit. Do not only listen on the outside, that is, to their words and opinions. The Holy Spirit will help you hear by imparting those gifts which are needed in the situation. Ask a few simple questions so that you are clear about the direction of your prayer. If it is apparent that you are out of your depth and you need help, then suggest this to the other person, find help and come back to the situation with the support and confidence of another more experienced Christian. If we yield our lives to the Lord every day, we will discover that by His gentle hand we will be led into all sorts of situations that are prepared by the Lord for us to move into prayer ministry.

S.D. Gordon said:

> 'Prayer is insisting on Jesus' victory and the retreat of the enemy on each particular spot. The enemy yields only what is taken. Therefore, ground must be taken step by step. Prayer must be definite.'

PART 10.6
The Laying On of Hands

As believers we can lay hands on other people in certain situations. Jesus laid hands on people in specific instances (Luke 13:13), and in the book of Acts we see that the church continued with that practice.

The laying on of hands has the following characteristics:

- it is a sign of identification with (as with the sin offering, Leviticus 1:4)

- it is to impart a blessing (Genesis 48:14–16)

- it signifies mutual commitment in Christ

We lay hands on other people when we pray for:

- the baptism of the Holy Spirit

- healing

- a blessing

- the gifts of the Holy Spirit

- the setting aside of someone to a position of ministry (this is to be done by leaders only)

- the anointing by the Holy Spirit

There are occasions when it is not advisable to lay hands on people, e.g. when there is demonic possession. An evil spirit must be dealt with in the Name of Jesus Christ and not with the laying on of hands.

When praying for others it is important always to ask God to protect you as well as the others. Ask for the protection of the Holy Spirit and to be covered by the blood of Jesus.

Pray simply and clearly and if the Holy Spirit tells you to say something specific to the other person, do so. Always remember that prayer ministry for others is spiritual warfare in action.

Personal Notes

Summary and Application

1. When we are praying, interceding for others, we need to be sure we are in a right place before God, fully equipped to resist the enemy.

2. Prayer links us to the unlimited possibilities of God.

3. Prayer in ministry is the application of God's power and blessing directly into people's lives.

4. To be effective when praying for others we need to be simple and clear in our approach and open to the leading and prompting of the Holy Spirit.

SECTION 11
Moving On in Faith

Introduction

Key Verses

Introduction

Without faith it is impossible to please God (Hebrews 11:6). None of us has the means within ourselves to meet God's demands or to fulfil the work of the Kingdom of God. We need a supernatural gift and that gift is the gift of faith. Faith is the power by which we come into new life in Jesus, and it is also the power by which this new life in God is going to develop. Everything is by faith!

This section will help us grow:

- in our personal life of faith

- in doing acts of faith, by exercising the special gift of faith

In John 6:28 the people asked:

'What must we do to do the works God requires?'

To which Jesus answered:

'The work of God is this: **to believe in the one He has sent.***'*

Faith is not a matter of the mind, but an act of the will (Proverbs 3:5). It means unwavering trust in God and His Word.

We are saved and born again through faith in Jesus Christ. This is the start of a continuing relationship of faith with God. There are many times that we need that special gift of faith; for example in our ministry, for decisions to be made, or for new circumstances. In this section we will discuss how we can grow in this special gift of faith, which is an extension of the relationship of faith between Father and child.

Jesus said:

'Everything is possible for him who believes.'

(Mark 9:23)

Faith opens us up to a capacity and potential that does not belong to our old human nature. A new world opens up to us – the Kingdom of God!

Key Verses

Romans 10:17   Luke 18:8

James 2:14–26   Mark 11:22–24

John 14:12   1 John 5:4

Hebrews 11:1–40   Mark 9:23

1 Corinthians 12:8–10

PART 11.1
Five Elements of Faith

F aith has a number of elements which are interrelated. It could be said that without any one of these five strands we have not fully expressed what faith is; nor can faith be fully operative in our lives when any one of them is missing. It is very important, therefore, to look for all these elements and to develop them.

i)   Faith is by *grace*

Faith is the very basis of our relationship with the Father. We are not saved through our own strength or righteousness, but by the grace of God (Ephesians 2:8–9). Unconsciously or not, we have been walking along in one direction in life, when suddenly God speaks. When we turn away from our old direction of life and listen instead to the Word of God, then the Holy Spirit brings something to us we did not have before – the gift of faith!

ii) Faith is *truth*

On a number of occasions the word *faith* appears in the New Testament with a definite article in front of it i.e. *the faith* (Jude 3). That tells us that there is something certain, clear and definite about this faith. It is not only important that we believe, but above all it is important what we believe. God's Word is the *truth*. This truth is the ground of our faith. Faith does not rest on a good idea, a philosophy or some emotional experience that we have, but on the Word of God.

iii) Faith is a *gift*

This gift of faith is for specific occasions and needs (1 Corinthians 12:9). It is this faith that looks at the impossible and cries, 'The God of heaven will give us success.'

This faith surpasses our understanding; it relies on a child-like dependency on God. It demands that we lay aside our own efforts and plans and throw ourselves afresh on our heavenly Father to give us the grace we need to help in time of need (Hebrews 4:16).

iv) Faith is a channel for God's *power*

Faith is vital, dynamic, effective and powerful.

Whenever we hear of faith in the Scriptures something powerful is happening, something powerful is shown (Acts 3:16). Jesus gave us some mighty, powerful promises of faith (e.g. John 14:12–14).

v) Faith is *victory*

Men of faith have always been those who have known the secret of how to overthrow the world's system (1 John 5:4). They have known how to withstand the enemies of God's Kingdom. Of course faith and obedience are closely linked. Faith enables us to believe God's Word and obedience prompts us to fulfil it.

PART 11.2
Faith and the Word of God

F aith and the Word of God go hand in hand. The Word of God creates faith and it calls for faith (Romans 10:17). Real faith depends on a word from God. This is true for our *normal* life of faith as a child of God as much as it is for specific circumstances in which we need a gift of faith. We cannot live in real faith until we hear the word of God for the situation. This word then creates faith in us and we can stand on it.

The Holy Spirit often uses Scriptures in situations of faith because once He has underlined them for us we can keep going back to them as God's promise to us. God's Word is trustworthy, because God is faithful (2 Timothy 2:11–13). Of course we can receive a word from God through other means, such as prophecy, visions, teaching etc., but this should always be compared with Scripture.

Standing in faith is an attitude that is taken in the light of a specific word from God in a specific situation. All the facts may not be clear, and certainly the way in which the word is going to be fulfilled is unlikely to be obvious at that moment. But faith knows! It has an inner understanding of the issue and a conviction of spirit that makes it certain of the outcome.

> '*Now faith is being sure of what we hope for and certain of what we do not see.*'   (Hebrews 11:1)

So the difference between *faith* and a *good idea* is the Word of God. This is an area where people may make mistakes, because they let their human desires and ambitions take control and lay claim to divine revelation when, in fact, they have no such thing. From the human level there is an element of risk attached to the life of faith.

PART 11.3
Five Things the Word of God Does for Us

i) It creates faith in us

Without the Word of God there is no faith. Faith is based on God's unchanging character (James 1:17; Psalm 9:10) and on His Word (Numbers 23:19).

ii) It prepares us for faith

The Word of God is powerful. It penetrates even to dividing soul and spirit, joints and marrow; it judges the thoughts and the attitudes of the heart (Hebrews 4:12). We need the Word of God for this judging between the thoughts and the attitudes of the heart. We need to develop thoughts and ideas in God and not *pies in the sky*, but we must not allow our thoughts to become set in concrete and so become rigid, unbending attitudes that we are unwilling to mature or change.

This means that the Word of God is able to reveal which acts are of the flesh and which are inspired by God. It is only the works of God that have life and produce life.

iii) It enables us in faith

The tremendous thing about the Word of God is that it provides us with an active alternative to all the negative thoughts and attitudes of our old nature. Our minds are so important to the life of faith. We are susceptible to all the impressions of our five senses. Satan tries to bring us into bondage to what is tangible and obvious. God's purpose is that we should be renewed in the attitudes of our minds (Romans 12:2). We need to stand in the living power of the Word of God.

iv) It directs us in faith

It is necessary for our faith that we are in the will of God and remain there. We need God's Word to direct us (Psalm 119:105; Isaiah 30:21), and we need wisdom to make the right decisions and to assess situations correctly (Proverbs 3:5–7).

v) It confirms faith in us

God will often give us a word that will enable us to continue in our stand of faith, to continue in the way He has shown us (2 Chronicles 20:20; Isaiah 7:9).

PART 11.4
Hindrances to Faith

- *Presumption* (Proverbs 3:5; Jeremiah 23:25–32)

- *Fear* (Mark 4:40; John 14:1)

- *Seeking glory and praise from men instead* (John 5:44)

- *Doubt* (James 1:6–8; Mark 11:23)

- *A guilty conscience* (1 John 3:21–22)

When we are standing in faith for any particular issue we can be sure that satan will try to hinder us. This he might do through factors which we would consider normal, without our recognising satan's influence. He will try and throw doubt on the Word of God – that is, he will try to mix a little bit of rationalism with faith. Or he will try feelings of weakness, unworthiness, darkness, despair, depression, hopelessness or even death.

For other hindrances refer to Section 9.4.

PART 11.5
Your God is Too Small

S atan knows that if we live with a diminished view of God then our faith will never rise to the need. God is alive and active. We have been put in touch with the God who made the universe.

> *'Is anything too hard for the Lord?'*   (Genesis 18:14)

> *'Is the Lord's arm too short? You will now see whether or not what I say will come true for you.'*
> (Numbers 11:23)

Faith is like a great experiment in God. Our faith level shows us the size of our God. God invites His people to put Him to the test (Malachi 3:10b). This is what faith is all about. The same mighty power which God used when He raised Jesus from the dead is available to us according to our faith (Matthew 15:28).

PART 11.6
You are Too Small

I f satan fails in his attack on our view of God he turns his attention to our view of ourselves. Many people live with such a poor self-image that they find faith impossible. Others, through circumstances, have been very discouraged. We need to enter into who we are in Christ.

The Bible says:

> *'Therefore, if anyone is in Christ, he is a new creation; the old has gone, the new has come!'* (2 Corinthians 5:17)

Reality is what God has done for us in Jesus. It is what God does, and will do for us, in the power of His Holy Spirit. Living in the good of your position in Christ helps you to escape from your poor self-image. It is not to try and pretend that the difficulties are not there, they are there all right – but to see ourselves as God does.

Faith is not illusion, not a *make believe*. The question that faith poses is this:

> *'Is there a higher truth than that which seems obvious at the moment?'*
> And faith cries, *'Yes, there is!* **that truth is God!'**

One example is Abraham. Against all hope, he in hope believed. To Abraham the promise was stronger than the fact of child-lessness. He looked beyond and listened to the promise of God (Romans 4:17–20).

Faith is always in the place of making a choice. We have to choose between two possibilities. What do we accept as truth?

- the things as they are, or seem to be? *or*
- the things that God has said; the things which are not seen but which God has promised?

> *'The one who is in you is greater than the one who is in the world.'* (1 John 4:4)

PART 11.7
Seven Steps to Effective Faith

i) Building our relationship with the Father

Trust in our heavenly Father is the basis of our faith. Anything that breaks this relationship breaks faith (1 John 3:21–22). At the heart of our faith needs to be an open relationship between God and us. Faith works best on a clean sheet, so we need to keep a daily account with our heavenly Father.

ii) Listening for God

Faith depends on hearing the Word of God. It is important to wait on the Word of God, to test it and to hold it, to ensure we are standing on faith ground. Once we have heard God's Word we can afford to wait for His answer no matter how long it takes.

iii) Ask in faith

Jesus taught:

> 'Ask and it will be given to you; seek and you will find; knock and the door will be opened to you.'
>
> (Luke 11:9)

Faith is knowing the will of God and simply coming in that knowledge before the Father to ask Him to work out His will. Many people pray not knowing. The most challenging and sometimes the most prolonged part of the faith exercise is not the asking in faith, but the process of becoming sure in faith.

iv) **Build your Ebenezers**

In the Old Testament, Ebenezers were stone pillars that were set up as witnesses to the help God had given (1 Samuel 7:12). These served as a testimony, for that generation and future generations, to the goodness of God. Faith builds on faith. This is why real men of faith cannot be shaken in their confidence in God. They can take you on a tour of their Ebenezers. It is encouraging to go and look again, in faith, at the things God has done for us in the past. They are there and they stand as indisputable witnesses to the goodness of God.

v) **Be filled with the Holy Spirit**

A powerful life of faith is a result of the Holy Spirit at work in us. Through the Holy Spirit God gives us:

- a revelation of Himself (John 14:15–24)

- a revelation of the truth (John 16:12–15)

- a revelation of His will (1 Corinthians 2:14–16)

- the prayer that is according to His will (Romans 8:26, 27)

- the gift of faith (1 Corinthians 12:9)

The other gifts of the Holy Spirit also contribute to the strengthening of our faith (1 Corinthians 12:7–11).

When we give room for the Holy Spirit, we will be able to say:

'If God is for us, who can be against us?'
(Romans 8:31)

Personal Notes

vi) Gain release from satan

It is necessary to claim God's resources for His own use. Satan tries to withhold what is rightfully God's. We need to learn how to prevail against the devil in praise and prayer to release these things from his hand. God created everything, but due to the fall everything has come under satan's dominion. On the cross Jesus paid the ransom. This includes everything, not just our sin; all things were created by Him and for Him (Colossians 1:15–20). In faith we stand on legal ground when reclaiming resources from satan. Fear is often a factor that prevents people from moving in faith. This is not from God (2 Timothy 1:7). We need to see that in Jesus we have been given authority to overcome the enemy and release the resources that are needed for His Kingdom in His name (Colossians 2:15; 3:17).

vii) Go back to the first word

In the period after receiving the assurance of faith we are often vulnerable to attack through seeds of confusion. At such times we need to go right back to the first word we received. God is not a God of confusion but of order. If you have real problems, then take your difficulty and share it with a person of faith whom you know you can trust.

Summary and Application

1. Faith releases God's power.

2. Faith is vertical trust, not horizontal belief.

3. To be a Christian believer means to be born in faith and born into faith. The challenge of Jesus is that we should be true to our birthright and live by faith.

4. Faith is given as a result of the Word of God being received into our lives.

5. Faith does not grow on the basis of self-effort, but rather through our looking to God (Hebrews 12:2; Mark 11:22).

6. The level of our faith shows the size of our God.

These points are as true for our daily lives of faith as God's children, as they are for those special moments in which God gives us His gift of faith.

Faith opens new possibilities in God, for God's possibilities are without limit. This is God's challenge for us. Do you personally know this life of faith?

The following Bible Study, **'Faith'**, will show us how we can grow in this.

Bible Study: *Faith*

Faith makes a channel between ourselves and God through which God's grace can come to us. Often faith is seen as something you have to work up yourself. This view has caused many Christians spiritual problems. We do not always have faith in circumstances like sickness for example, and this may cause us to feel guilty.

Faith is not something you have at the tip of your fingers, it is a gift from God and the result of an intimate relationship with our heavenly Father. In this study we will take a closer look at the principles of faith.

1. In Hebrews 11:1–3 we find a description of faith. Read these verses and then paraphrase them in your own words:

    _____

    _____

    _____

    _____

    _____

2. Through faith we receive many blessings. Read the verses mentioned below and write down the blessing found in each verse:

    a) Romans 5:1 _____

        _____

        _____

    b) Romans 6:8; Galatians 2:20 _____

        _____

        _____

c) Matthew 9:22 _____

_____

_____

d) John 7:37, 38 _____

_____

_____

3. Question 2 shows us some blessings of faith. Now for the opposite. Write down the results of unbelief mentioned in the following verses:

a) Deuteronomy 1:30–36 _____

_____

_____

b) Mark 4:40 _____

_____

_____

c) Hebrews 4:2 _____

_____

_____

d) Mark 16:16 _____

_____

_____

e) Matthew 13:58 _____

_____

_____

4.   Unbelief is a serious thing. It makes it impossible for God to give us that which He would love us to have. Moreover, it does not glorify God.

Read Hebrews 11:6a and describe how we can please God:

_____

_____

Complete the quotation of verse 6b below:

'*Because anyone who comes to him* [God] *must*

_____

and that he _____ *those who*

_____ .'

5.   1 John 5:4 says very clearly that we can only overcome through:

_____

_____

Victory is through faith. Which earnest question did Jesus ask in Luke 18:8?

_____

_____

Why did Jesus ask this question? (see verses 1–7)

_____

_____

_____

What was the disciples' cry of distress in Luke 17:5?

_____

_____

What was Jesus trying to say in verse 6?

_____

_____

_____

Jesus taught his disciples to live and work by faith. He told them not to be overly concerned with the measure of their faith; the essential questions were:

- In **Whom** *did they believe?*

- **What** would they do with their faith?

6. The most important thing is to know in **Whom** we believe, as it is possible to believe in other gods or *truths*.

Jesus clearly teaches us in Whom we should believe, see John 6:29. We should believe in:

_____

_____

Faith rests in Jesus Christ. This is true for our ministry as much as for our salvation. It is quite possible to continue in our own strength after we have been born again.

How is Jesus' work on earth being carried on, according to John 14:12 and Colossians 3:17?

_____

_____

_____

_____

Personal faith in Jesus opens a channel for His work, in and through our lives, by the power of the Holy Spirit.

Personal Notes

7. If our ministry is to grow, then our faith in Jesus should grow. How do we make our faith grow?

    a) ***Be honest***
        Read Mark 9:24. What was the father's prayer?

        _____

        _____

        Do not assume that you have faith when you do not. Assuming something can be a big obstacle for faith.

    b) ***Make it your aim to glorify God***
        Read John 5:44. What other obstacle is there for faith?

        _____

        _____

        Tell God your Father that you are completely dependent on Him, that you cannot do it your-self. Be honest and consider your motivation. Is your aim to glorify God?

    c) ***Be pure of heart***
        Read Psalm 24:3, 4 and Matthew 5:8. Faith develops because of a revelation from God. What precondition is there?

        _____

        _____

    d) ***Read God's Word***
        Read Romans 10:17. How does one get faith?

        _____

        _____

        Faith comes through the Word and develops through the Word.

e) ***Be obedient***
Read James 2:17 and 4:17. What does faith mean in the practice of daily living?

_____

_____

_____

When God gives us faith we must put it into practice; not in our own strength, but in God's strength. That is what faith is all about.

8. There is often a problem between points d) and e) of the previous question. When should we do what God asks us to do and how?

As believers we can tip the scales in two directions:

* ***Activity***: being legalistic, doing works only

* ***Passivity***: being passive, not doing any works at all

Neither of them is right. So what should we do?

Galatians 5:6 gives the answer. Read it, and fill in the blanks:

'*The only thing that counts is faith,* _____

_____ . '

The love of God liberates us from a legalistic way of life and from a life of passivity; instead it gives us power for our faith to express itself through love.

We must begin by asking God for love and compassion (Romans 5:5; 2 Corinthians 5:14).

9. In Hebrews 12:2 we are being exhorted to continue in our faith. Faith has everything to do with making choices, it demands commitment. Now go to God in prayer and make a decision for Him, telling Him that from now on you will not do things in your own strength; from now on you will put your faith in Him, the One who has all power.

    Summarise your prayer below:

    _____

    _____

    _____

    _____

Answers

1. Personal

2. a) Peace with God.
    b) Sharing in the death and resurrection life of Christ.
    c) The woman was healed.
    d) Being filled with the Holy Spirit.

3. a) They were not allowed to enter the promised land.
    b) The disciples were afraid and fearful.
    c) The Word has no power in your life.
    d) Unbelief will result in the judgement of God.
    e) Jesus cannot do any miracles.

4. Faith pleases God; we give Him pleasure by believing that He can do all things because He is almighty. It pleases God when we trust Him fully and obey Him. This will glorify Him.

    See Bible

5. Faith.

    When the Son of Man comes, will He find faith on the earth?

    To show them that they should not give up praying in faith.

    Increase our faith.

    That they should use their faith, however small.

    A small faith in a great God works miracles.

6. In the one God has sent; this is Jesus.

    By faith in Jesus Christ and doing deeds in His name.

7. a) 'I believe. Help me in my unbelief!' This father was honest and did not assume he had faith when he did not have it.
    b) Looking for praise for yourself, pride.
    c) Holiness, a pure heart.
    d) Through hearing the Word.
    e) Having faith is being obedient and doing deeds in the power of God.

8. expressing itself through love.

9. Personal

Introduction

I n this chapter we will study the grace and anointing of God and what this mean to us as believers. We cannot do anything for God unless we have experienced His grace and we know and operate in His anointing. In fact, grace and anointing go hand-in-hand, because they are both sourced in God and reveal just how dependent on God we really are.

When we speak about anointing there seems to be no difference between that and being filled with the Holy Spirit – yet there is. The baptism of the Holy Spirit is for every believer and serves to make our lives of faith dynamic, to produce the fruit of the Spirit and to give us the gifts of the Spirit. The anointing releases the gift and causes it to be effective in ministry. This is different for every believer and is determined by God.

The *grace* of God opens the way and the *anointing* of God gives us the ability to fulfil God's will.

Key Verses

2 Corinthians 1:21, 22	1 Samuel 16:1–13
1 John 2:20, 27	Isaiah 61:1
Acts 13:2–4	Luke 4:18, 19

PART 12.1
The Outworking of Grace

In 1 Corinthians 15:10 Paul says the following:

> *'By the grace of God I am what I am, and His grace to me was not without effect. No, I worked harder than all of them – yet not I, but the grace of God that was with me.'*

The grace of God is the foundation for:

- our salvation and our life of faith
- our service for Him

As Christians we should be controlled by the grace God has given us. We receive God's grace by living in His will. This grace then gives us the potential to carry out the will of God. The grace of God, however, is only made effective when we move forward in faith. In other words, we first need to know God's will, we then need to receive the grace of God for that will to be accomplished, and finally we need to step out in practical ways in order for the will of God to be achieved.

God equips everyone with His anointing to be able to carry out His will. This anointing makes God's grace effective and it produces fruit in us and in the lives of those to whom we minister (John 15:1–16), proving that we are called and gifted by God.

PART 12.2
What is God's Anointing?

The main Hebrew word translated *anoint* in the New International Version of the Bible is **mashach** which means *to apply oil by smearing, pouring or spreading*. The Hebrew word **masiah**, transliterated *messiah*, means *anointed one* and it seems to be derived from this word.

In the Old Testament times the anointing of God was often symbolised by pouring oil onto the person. This sacred use of oil was for the anointing of things or people in order to consecrate them to God (Genesis 28:18). For example; for priests (Exodus 28:41), for kings (1 Samuel 10:1) and for prophets (1 Kings 19:16). Once anointed with oil these people were considered chosen and set apart to carry out His specific service.

The two main Greek words translated as *anoint* in the New International Version of the Bible are **aleipho** which was a general term for anointing of any kind, and **crio**, which is more limited in its usage because it is confined to sacred or symbolic anointings. Both words simply mean *the rubbing* or *spreading of oil, perfume* or *ointment*. The title *Christ* uses the second word and it means *The Anointed One* (Isaiah 61:1; Luke 4:19).

The early church may not have anointed people physically with oil to set them apart for a specific service, but they did lay hands on them to do this. It could be said that the laying on of hands in the New Testament replaced anointing with oil used in the Old Testament, because they both symbolically represent the impartation of the anointing of God and a consecration of the people to Him.

In summary, the anointing of God can be defined as God pouring His Holy Spirit onto and into our lives for a specific service, enabling us to serve God with His power and so impart His life into the lives of those with whom we come into contact.

PART 12.3
The Importance of God's Anointing

A leader in God's church without His anointing will be unable to produce any lasting fruit. The anointing of the Holy Spirit, rather than natural personality, ability, eloquence, training or gifting, is the source of true effectiveness for God. This anointing of God gives power to our work, authority to our words, freshness to our presentation, and relevance to our actions. This anointing is an essential, indispensable prerequisite for all God's leaders.

> *'This is the word of the Lord to Zerubbabel: "Not by might, nor by power, but by my Spirit," says the Lord Almighty.'* (Zechariah 4:6)

When the early church needed people to wait on tables and look after the widows they looked for people who were full of the Spirit and wisdom in order to meet the need (Acts 6:1–6). Leaders such as this have an abundance that makes them a source of supply to other people.

PART 12.4
The Source of God's Anointing

Our anointing flows out of our relationship with God and the call He has laid on our lives. God is the source of the anointing (John 15:1–17). If we want to know the anointing of God we must stay inside His call on our lives. This is also true with the specific details of how we out-work that call. We need God's specific anointing on each aspect of our work for Him.

God wants to deal with His leaders deeply. These people live holy lives before God because they do not want to do anything that will dishonour Him who has done so much for them. They will obey God because they know Him, they know how much He loves them and they understand that He wants only the best for them. It is upon such people that God can pour out His anointing, because the anointing will not remain just with them, but will enable and empower them to achieve God's will.

PART 12.5
Releasing God's Anointing

We need to know how to flow with the anointing, and never try to force or strive in it. We do, however, always need to stay available to God. God will make the anointing available to us at the right time and we need to be open to it. We must begin to learn the keys in ourselves that will release us to the anointing of the Holy Spirit within us. These keys will be different for different people.

Some keys people have found to be effective include:

- worship

- prayer and fasting

- meditating on God, who He is

- praise

- being prayed for by other people you trust

- receiving a specific *word* from God for the situation into which you are about to minister

- being still and silent before God and waiting on Him

- reading appropriate parts of God's Word

There are probably many other ways of making ourselves available to the anointing of God. A lot depends on our personality and the situation in which we find ourselves at any particular time. The right thing to do is to discover what works for you, making sure you never resort to a rigid formula into which the Holy Spirit has no chance of breaking.

PART 12.6
Increasing Our Anointing

The anointing is only increased as we:

- prove faithful in the small things God ask us to do for Him.

- give sacrificially of ourselves and our possessions to God. The anointing of God costs every leader something, and the deeper we go with Him the more He will ask us to give up.

- get to know more of God by entering into His presence more frequently and entering more deeply into the ministry of prayer and worship. After all, the anointing is sourced in God.

- are broken before God.

- appreciate and guard the anointing which has been made available to us.

PART 12.7
We Still Need to Prepare

The anointing of God does not negate the need for us to prepare both our life and our material. To become a craftsman of the Word of God requires discipline, study, diligence, perseverance and application.

There are leaders who only lean on their preparation. This also is wrong. We need to get the right balance between those two important aspects of Christian ministry: preparation and anointing. This balance will vary according to the situation, our maturity in Christ, our level of knowledge of the Word of God, the type of leader we are, our experience, and what God wants to do in that particular situation.

PART 12.8
The Laying On of Hands to Receive God's Anointing

The Scriptures urge us not to be too hasty in the laying on of hands, because to acclaim someone prematurely as leader by this action can be dangerous both to the church and to the individual involved (1 Timothy 5:22). This verse mainly refers to the setting aside of someone to a position of ministry or eldership in the church. It is necessary, first of all, to see evidence that God is leading a person into a place of ministry before we set them apart to that work. It is also important that we only raise up a person in God's timing (1 Timothy 3:6). It is a serious matter to have someone whom God has not called in a position of leadership in His Church.

The laying on of hands is for the identification, impartation and releasing of a person's ministry, the impartation of spiritual gifts; the consecration of these people to the Lord and His work and the receiving of the anointing of God (Acts 6:6; 13:2, 3; 1 Timothy 4:14; 2 Timothy 1:6).

It must be remembered that although only anointed leaders in a church should lay hands on those who are being raised up into leadership, the anointing does not come from the leaders, but from God. The laying on of hands is a sign. The people on whom hands are laid will not automatically receive God's anointing, but must look to the Lord in faith to receive it. To receive anything good from the Lord requires faith.

PART 12.9
Results of God's Anointing

- It enables and empowers us in our work for God. The anointing of God enhances and extends our normal human capabilities and capacities if we consecrate them to Him. It enables us to achieve far more as a human servant of God than we could do without it (2 Corinthians 3:4–6).

- It enables us to produce fruit that will last for God.

- It confirms that we have God's authority. When we, and others, see signs of the anointing of God on our lives, we know that He has delegated His authority to us and is confirming our ministry in the situation. In fact authority can be thought of as the twin brother of anointing. One without the other is devastating.

- It reveals God's unfailing kindness and faithfulness to His anointed ones (Psalm 18:50). God will not ask His people to do something for Him and not make available to them everything they need in order to do that thing.

- It reveals the heart of God, because He will only do what is consistent with His character and what He has revealed of it in His Word.

- It enables us to rest in God, to be truly free and to know His peace. This takes much of the striving out of serving God. His yoke is easy and His burden is light (Matthew 11:28–30). With the anointing of God, we, as leaders, can gladly take up the responsibility He has given to us.

- It brings with it sensitivity to the needs of people, thus enabling us to respond in a compassionate and loving way. It helps us to see and do what Jesus would do in the situation. This can result in saying the right word or receiving insight into what to pray for, and the gifts of the Spirit being shown.

- It teaches us the truth about all things and it teaches us to remain in Jesus Christ (1 John 2:20, 27). This is a universal anointing for the whole Church.

- It enables us to see things as God sees them and to have His insight, wisdom, understanding and discernment. These things are not given for our own sake, but to enable us to serve God more effectively.

- It will stimulate others. As we function in our anointing, it will enable those we lead to come into their anointing.

- It brings the presence and power of God into any situation.

PART 12.10
Things That Can Destroy God's Anointing

L eaders will, at times, be astonished what they can accomplish for God when they function in His anointing. Without it they could not do what God wanted them to do and so would be impotent in the face of the needs He brought to their attention. There is little that is more frustrating than seeing a need we are unable to meet. God's leaders should, therefore, be careful not to do anything to hinder His anointing. They certainly should do nothing that will cause Him to withdraw it. The thought of losing the anointing God has given to us should motivate us to continue to obey Him and live righteous lives that are pleasing to Him.

It is devastating to lose one's anointing. There are examples in Scripture of people who lost their anointing, e.g. Samson and Saul.

There are *universal* things which can undo the anointing, such as:

- *Sin*
  When we sin or give ourselves to the things of the world, God may still be able to work through us to some extent, but we will not be able to live in the full blessing and anointing of God.

- *Disunity*
  Especially among a church's leaders. God can only command His blessing where there is unity (Psalm 133:1–3).

- *Unbelief*
  This makes God's anointing ineffective, because it is the opposite of faith. God can only work in response to faith (Mark 6:4–6).

- *An ungodly atmosphere*
  When there is an atmosphere of unbelief or oppression, the anointing of God will be hindered. We need to resist the enemy at such times.

- *Fear*

  Fear seeks to dominate our lives. If we let it do so, it will destroy our courage and render us ineffective. We need to fear God but nothing else, especially not the opinions of other people (2 Timothy1:7; 1 John 4:18).

- *Spiritual lethargy*

  This is being idle and not bothering to do what we know we should be doing in God. Some of the causes of this include: being disillusioned, frustration, disappointment, failure, defeat and laziness.

- *Tiredness*

  This can put us in a bad frame of mind and cause us to fail to tap into our anointing by waiting on God. He is the source of our refreshment and strength.

- *Aggravation*

  When we are angry, or even irritated, we will find that we cannot minister effectively to other people. We must be on our guard and resist the enemy so as to prevent him from gaining victory in our life. We also need to forgive anyone who may have wronged us, no matter how right we are (Matthew 6:14, 15).

- *Hurt, disappointment, failure and discouragement*

  All these things tend to cause us to lose confidence in ourselves and in what God can do through us. We need to come to God and increase our faith by meeting with Him and hearing His word to us. We need to learn how to step over our difficulties and to always live in victory.

Then there are *specific* things that can undo our anointing:

- *Presuming on the anointing*
  God wants His people to look to Him continually and
  never to presume that He will do as He has done in the
  past. We need to wait on God and make this our life-style.
  Even the Son of God, Jesus, had to do this and we are to
  follow His example (1 John 2:6).

- *Not living in our anointing*
  We can do this by denying our anointing and living as if it
  is not there; by trying to attain our goals by human effort.

- *Confusing position with anointing*
  Strong leaders need to be broken before God. They need to
  learn what counts in the Kingdom of God. Effectiveness in
  the Kingdom of God is not counted in the number of
  people following us, but in how well we obey God and do
  His will (Matthew 7:21–23).

- *Confusing emotionalism with anointing*
  A good communicator will be able to get an emotional
  response from people, especially when they are speaking to
  a crowd. However, emotions wear off, and the people who
  have responded to an emotional appeal tend to quickly go
  back to what they were and did before. When people meet
  with God's anointing they are meeting with God, and this
  will have the lasting impact on their lives.

- *Relying on natural abilities or talents instead of on God*
  Our natural talents and abilities are not wrong in themselves, they just need to be consecrated to God so He can
  anoint them. They will then be very fruitful and effective
  tools in His service.

- *By using a professional and secular approach*
  God can only move in power when we do His will in His
  way. Trying to do things the way the world does them, or
  using professionalism or gimmicks as a substitute for God's
  anointing, is doomed to failure. That way it is not God but
  man who gets the glory.

- *Using the anointing for our own ends*

  If we seek to gain fame, power, wealth, position, respect, etc. from our anointing instead of giving all the glory to God, we are in danger of not only losing our anointing, but also incurring God's wrath and severe judgement. We should never dishonour God by despoiling the anointing He has given us in this way. We must also never glorify what the anointing enables us to achieve, more than we glorify God.

- *Believing it is unnecessary*

  Many Christians have relegated the working of the Holy Spirit largely to the first century. Therefore they do not look to Him for the empowering and enabling to do God's work. Instead they battle in their own strength, according to their own opinion and expectations, and do the best they can.

  When we limit ourselves in that way to what we know, see and do, then we have excluded faith in God's anointing.

Application of the Course

1. The objective of our lives is to *love* (Matthew 22:36–40).

   This also applies to the church; read Revelation 2:1–7, and describe the danger of doing things without love:

   _____

   _____

   _____

   _____

   In 2 Corinthians 5:14 Paul explains his motivation for serving Christ. Is this your desire as well?

   ○ Yes

   ○ No

2. *Brokenness* is an essential ingredient for a ministry in the power of God. If there is no brokenness, no dying to our own fleshly power, we will continue to use it and there will be no openness for the power of the Holy Spirit.

   Describe the principle seen in the grain of wheat in John 12:24:

   _____

   _____

   _____

   Do you experience this in your own life?

   ○ Yes

   ○ No

3. God wants to use us as channels for the work of the Holy Spirit. We would not think of putting clean water in a dirty glass, would we? Neither would God want to pour His Holy Spirit into lives that are not clean. *Holiness* is a prerequisite for a pure ministry in the power of the Holy Spirit. Is this your desire and do you pray for it?

    O   Yes

    O   No

    God sanctifies us through His fire (Matthew 3:11). This implies that there are things in our lives that have to pass through the fire. Describe the things that you find hard to put on the altar:

    _____

    _____

    _____

    _____

4. In our ministry we are dealing with a spiritual enemy and this means *spiritual warfare*. Most of the battle takes place within ourselves. In James 4:1–8 we read about this.

    What is the source of this struggle according to verse 1?

    _____

    _____

    And what is the result (verses 2 and 3)?

    _____

    _____

    _____

    What is the exhortation given in verse 7?

    _____

    _____

And what is the promise?

_____

_____

5. God wants to equip us with the *gifts of the Spirit*.

a) Do you long for the gifts?

○ Yes

○ No

b) Have you ever experienced that, at a certain moment, God gave you a particular gift?

○ Yes

○ No

c) Have you discovered your own particular gift which God has given you?

○ Yes

○ No

If so, which gift is it? _____

d) Are you open for a service ministry within your church, or in missions? Even if this is *full-time* work?

○ Yes

○ No

e) Is your gift or ministry growing?

○ Yes

○ No

f) Does your intimate relationship with God have first place here?

○ Yes

○ No

Personal Notes

6. *Prayer* is an absolute must for a powerful ministry. Prayer links us to the unlimited possibilities of God.

   a) Does personal prayer have first priority in your service ministry?

      ○ Yes

      ○ No

      If not, why not?

      _____

      _____

   b) Have you ever prayed for someone else where God allowed you to be a channel through which His blessing could flow towards the person you prayed for? (e.g. in a time of ministry)

      ○ Yes

      ○ No

7. Prayer links us with the unlimited possibilities of God and His promises. However, we need *faith* to see God's possibilities and promises become reality. Faith serves as a channel between the blessing that God wants to give from heaven, and the need here on earth. Through faith the Kingdom of God becomes manifest in and through our lives.

   Read about Abraham's battle of faith in Romans 4:18–22, and summarise it below:

   _____

   _____

   _____

Proclaimers International is an international Christian ministry led by Dr Bob Gordon and based at Drayton Hall, Norwich, UK.

Dr Gordon is a prophetic teacher, preacher and author who has written a number of books on key issues in spiritual life.

The aim of Proclaimers International is to serve the wider Body of Christ and has three major emphases; Leadership, Discipleship and Evangelism in the power of the Holy Spirit. These elements of the ministry are expressed in the various strands of the work.

- **Proclaimers Spirit and Word School.** Full-time and part-time training courses are held continuously at Drayton Hall and welcome students from all over the world. The full-time course lasts for one year and consists of three terms. Students may attend all or part of the course which runs on a modular basis. The part-time course lasts for two years and is held one day a week. The School also offers distance learning courses which are available as printed material, computer diskette, audio tape or email.

- **Proclaimers Network.** An important networking of leadership, mainly in the UK, but some overseas. This Network is aimed at stimulating and encouraging leadership and providing a forum for discussion and spiritual insight on issues of contemporary significance.

  Proclaimers Network functions through a series of Forums held occasionally through the year at Drayton Hall and by means of a quarterly house journal, *Proclaimers*, which provides a practical link between leaders and provides articles of interest and challenge.

- **Proclaimers Resources.** A wide range of books, videos and audio cassettes are offered by Dr Gordon and other authors and speakers which reflect the heart of the ministry. These are available by Mail Order. Please see the main advert for details.

- **Conference Programme.** Throughout the year a diary of Special Conferences is held at Drayton Hall usually led by Dr Bob Gordon or other well known speakers. Full details of this programme can be obtained direct from Proclaimers International.

- **The King's Coach.** A unique evangelistic ministry which operates in other countries as well as Britain. This ministry operates with specially built vehicles which present the Gospel through a vibrant and interesting exhibition and also provide an area for personal meeting and counselling. The King's Coach operates in Europe and New Zealand as well as the UK.

- **Proclaimers International Ministries.** Linked with bases in the Netherlands, Germany, Uganda and New Zealand, which reflect the teaching and evangelistic ministry of Proclaimers International.

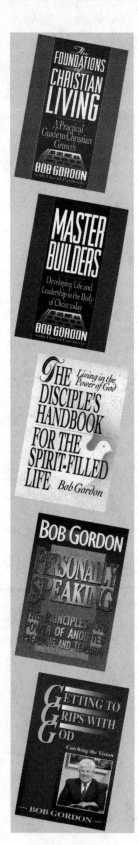

Foundations of Christian Living

This book has been written to help a wide range of Christians, from new believers to leaders of all kinds. It provides a practical, systematic study-guide to the fundamental principles of discipleship which will stimulate growth towards maturity. This book has made a terrific impact in many nations and has been translated into several major languages.

Master Builders

A valuable resource written especially for leaders and designed to encourage maturity and effectiveness within Christian leadership. It offers a 30 part study-guide which presents a balanced view of leadership with a clear, practical and spiritual challenge to all who desire to grow in spiritual responsibility within the Body of Christ.

The Disciple's Handbook for the Spirit-filled Life

This handbook teaches us about following Jesus in every part of our lives. Nine major sections focus upon key areas of Christian faith and experience: Discipleship, The Cross, God's Word, Faith, Fruitfulness, Authority, Spiritual Warfare, Ministry and the Holy Spirit.

Personally Speaking

Prophetic preaching is on the agenda again. The Word and the Spirit are the two main agencies by which God performs His purposes on earth. This book explores some important principles with regard to the dynamic revelation of the Word and the operations of the Spirit in inspiring and empowering human beings to share words of divine power.

Getting to Grips with God – A two video series

1. *Catching the Vision*. The two sessions on this video could change your life! They deal with the subject of spiritual vision and its implications for our life and work. For every Christian, as God wants to show each of us how to serve Him more effectively and how this can transform the most seemingly mundane and trivial task.

2. *Going for Gold*. A natural successor to *Catching the Vision*. The book of Proverbs tells us to guard our hearts for much of what holds us back is within – we need to take control of our inner lives in the power of God. Freedom in the Spirit requires that we be good stewards of our life and time. Bob Gordon gives some practical help to all who want to make life and time more effective in God's service.

For further information please contact:

Help Desk, Proclaimers International
Drayton Hall, Drayton
Norwich NR8 6DP
England

or visit our web site:

http://www.proclaim.org.uk